Alcoholism

MODERN MONOGRAPHS IN INDUSTRIAL MEDICINE   **2**

Editor in Chief: ANTHONY J. LANZA, M.D.
Consulting Editor: RICHARD H. ORR, M.D.

Alcoholism

By ARNOLD Z. PFEFFER, M.D.

Formerly Associate Clinical Professor
of Psychiatry, College of Medicine
of New York University, In charge,
Consultation Clinic for Alcoholism
New York University-Bellevue
Medical Center

GRUNE & STRATTON   •   1958

NEW YORK AND LONDON

Contents

Introduction

ALCOHOLISM is the book his colleagues have wanted Dr. Arnold Z. Pfeffer to write. Clearly, concisely and logically are recorded here the results and conclusions derived from analytical psychiatric research in the field of alcoholism and addictive diseases, beginning in 1942 at the United States Public Health Service hospital for addiction at Lexington, Kentucky. By training and temperament, Dr. Pfeffer was the ideal choice for Director of the Consultation Clinic for Alcoholism at the University Hospital of the New York University-Bellevue Medical Center, sponsored in 1952 by the Consolidated Edison Company of New York. This clinic, the first ever to be devoted exclusively to the alcoholic in industry, evolved from the progressive and far reaching policy of the Consolidated Edison Company which was started in 1947. It is dedicated to the proposition that alcoholism is a serious medical condition both in and out of industry and that alcoholics are sick people in need of and deserving study and treatment. The combination of this policy backed up by a specialized clinic in a great University Medical Center symbolized the end of ancient superstitutions, prejudices and misconceptions about alcoholism and alcoholics.

Little or no medical cognizance of alcoholism was taken until Dr. Benjamin Rush first wrote of it as a medical problem in 1785. As early as 1830 a committee of the Connecticut Medical Society issued a report calling for the establishment of a rehabilitation facility for alcoholics—stressing the failure of the then current method of sending them to jails or workhouses—and urging research into causes, effects and treatment of alcoholism. But over a century passed with little or nothing accomplished until 1935 when an alcoholic layman searched for and found an alcoholic physician in Akron, Ohio. Together they founded the fellowship of Alcoholics Anonymous thereby sparking renewed interest in the disease of alcoholism which, according to a recent survey (1957) of the National Better Business Bureau, costs business and industry over a billion dollars a year in absenteeism and labor turnover alone—thus "the billion dollar hangover" appellation. In 1944, Yale University established the Yale Plan Clinic for Alcohol Studies and the National Council on Alcoholism began its tripartite program sponsoring education, service facilities and research on alcoholism. Alcoholism is now considered to be one of the nation's leading public health problems, outranked probably only by mental illness, cardiovascular disease and cancer. Finally, in 1956, a resolution of the American Medical Association, stating that alcoholics are valid patients, and should be treated as such, was unanimously passed by its House of Delegates.

It has been said that alcoholism is a subtle and unique disease about which we know less than we do about pneumonia, only as much perhaps as we do about cancer. Possibly for the very reason that alcoholism is a unique disease with its subtle interplay of psychological, physiological, and sociological factors, we have had such difficulty understanding it. ALCOHOLISM is a magnificent reservoir of new and useful knowledge, particularly of the psychological and psychiatric aspects of the disease, relating not only to the alcoholic in industry but wherever he may be and he not only may be but is likely to be everywhere.

Harold W. Lovell, M.D.
Clinical Professor, New York Medical College;
President, National Council on Alcoholism

Foreword

In RECENT YEARS industry has become increasingly aware of the need to deal constructively with the employee who has a drinking problem. Industry's attitude is changing from the consideration of alcoholism as exclusively a social and personal problem to the realization that this disorder is a medical condition, within certain limitations, as much as diabetes or heart disease. In common with other sick people, the alcoholic cannot help himself without outside assistance. There are some qualifications to the consideration of alcoholism as a disease, because there is a personal element in the development of the condition and it is especially important that there be a willingness on the part of the individual to accept treatment. This concept forms the basis of the industrial approach to problem drinking, which essentially sets up a procedure for probation to motivate the employee to do something constructive about his drinking problem and couples it with a medical program for rehabilitation.

The forthright recognition of problem drinking in industry together with a program for rehabilitation has proved worthwhile. The reports from many companies indicate that an increasing number of employees have been restored to economic usefulness and case absenteeism has been reduced. The good results of industrial programs demonstrate that such efforts yield material rewards in salvaging the skill and experience of long-service employees and contribute to an overall improvement in employee relations. These programs are a positive step toward the prevention of disability from chronic problem drinking.

S. C. Franco, M.D., F.A.C.P.
Associate Medical Director,
Consolidated Edison Company of New York, Inc.

Preface

THIS MONOGRAPH is intended to serve physicians as a handbook for the management of alcoholic patients. It is especially aimed at the needs of the physician in industry where the occupational features of alcoholism are more easily seen. Though the problem of medical management is essentially the same for industrial physicians as it is for others, there are certain areas in which the problem is highlighted. The industrial physician is in a notably advantageous position to help motivate the alcoholic to seek assistance.

The problem of alcoholism has been with us since man learned about fermentation and it is even mentioned in the Bible. However, it has only been in the past fifteen years that medicine has directed a more intense interest toward the specific laboratory and clinical problems of this illness, and only in the past ten years have various industries approached it with vigor.

Alcoholism is a complicated disease touching on a multiplicity of disciplines—biochemistry, physiology, and pathology of various systems, especially the gastrointestinal and nervous systems. There are also important psychiatric, social and cultural implications. Most physicians are confronted with some aspect of alcoholism in their work, and it is hoped that this volume will provide a practical orientation to this complex medical problem.

The volume of medical literature on the various facets of alcoholism is large and the points of view are numerous and diverse. The goal of this volume is to present those concepts and treatment procedures that have borne the test of extensive practical application.

Exacting studies of the number of alcoholics in industry are lacking, but conservative statistical estimates based on the results of spot surveys indicate that 2,060,000 alcoholics are regularly employed; 1,370,000 alcoholic males are employed in manufacturing plants, by construction companies and public utilities.[1] At the Consolidated Edison Company (New York) there is an average of forty new cases of problem drinking each year in a group of approximately 20,000 employees—an annual incidence of one and one-half to two new cases per thousand employees

---

[1] Jellinek, E. M., What shall we do about alcoholism? Vital Speeches 13: 252–253, 1947.

per year. Experience with disability evaluation of chronic medical conditions indicates that the actual incidence of alcoholism in industry is probably two per cent. However, cases of problem drinking may be hidden even in companies with an established alcoholism program.[2]

The male alcoholic in industry loses an average of 22 working days annually (as compared with 7.5 days for the non-alcoholic), a total of 29,700,000 working days. The alcoholic has an accident rate that is twice as high as the non-alcoholic, and life span is reduced approximately twelve years in contrast to that of the non-alcoholic or ordinary drinker.[1]

A severe loss to industry occurs when an experienced worker or executive is dismissed because of drinking. An analysis in a heavy industry [3] of records of 338 employees disciplined for drinking shows:

Years of Service	Number of Employees
1–4 years	127
5–9 years	84
10–14 years	55
15–19 years	31
25 years and over	20

Estimates of the cost to industry of alcoholism among employees are staggering. The direct costs of alcoholism are related to man-hours lost through absenteeism charged to "illness," medical expenses, accidents, disability payments, and pension payments to alcoholics who are retired prematurely. Indirect costs of alcoholism arise from inefficiency among alcoholics and a slowdown in production when an alcoholic is part of a production team.

The alcoholic in industry is essentially the same as the alcoholic elsewhere. However, as will be indicated in CHAPTER VII of this volume, results of industrial programs in the rehabilitation of alcoholics have been remarkably good as compared with results in other groups. This undoubtedly stems from the fact that employees who have been able to maintain many years of employment at the same company tend as a group to be relatively more stable. In addition, they tend to be better motivated for treatment and abstinence in relation to the possi-

[2] Franco, S. C., Problem drinking in industry. Review of a company program. Indust. Med. & Surg. *26:* 221–228, 1957.

[3] O'Brien, R., Alcoholism among disciplinary cases in industry. Quart. J. Stud. Alcohol *10:* 268, 1949.

bility of losing valued jobs and benefits. Because of these features, there is in industry a pool of alcoholics with better than usual prognosis. Thus, industry is in a unique position to assist in the rehabilitation of these sick people and to thereby bring credit and advantages to itself in salvaging valuable personnel.

The plan of this volume is, first, to present an orientation to alcoholism as a disease, including definition, etiology and a general discussion of complications, diagnosis, prognosis and treatment. As for etiology, it is concluded that psychological factors are central. The details of the medical and neuropsychiatric complications of alcoholism are the topics of CHAPTERS II and III respectively. CHAPTER IV concerns itself with some of the details of the psychology of the alcoholic. This is followed in CHAPTER V by a discussion of psychological treatments, Alcoholics Anonymous and, from the point of view of treatability—the important problem of motivation. In CHAPTER VI hospitalization and Antabuse are considered as adjunctive treatments and procedures. Also included are brief discussions of some treatments of less certain value. The last part of the volume is devoted to a description of industrial programs for alcoholics. One plan, the Consolidated Edison-New York University-Bellevue Plan, is discussed in detail. In this discussion, many of the medical and psychological problems taken up in previous sections are seen in actual application to the special industrial setting. Programs of large and small companies and additional sources of assistance are also taken up in the final two chapters.

Appreciation is expressed to Drs. Daniel J. Feldman and Sidney S. Greenberg for their assistance in the preparation of the sections on medical and neurologic complications and to Dr. E. M. Jellinek for permission to quote parts of his article, "Phases of Alcohol Addiction," that appeared in the Quarterly Journal of Studies on Alcoholism (*13:* 673–684, 1952). Some of this material was first published in brief form in 1950 in Veteran's Administration Technical Bulletin (TB 10–67) in collaboration with Dr. S. Bernard Wortis.

—The Author

I   *An Orientation to Alcoholism as a Disease*

THE PURPOSE of this chapter is to present a general orientation to the disease, alcoholism, under the headings of: (a) Definition, (b) Etiology, (c) Medical and Personal Consequences, (d) Diagnosis, (e) Prognosis, and (f) Treatment. Detailed elaboration of the psychological etiology and consequences of alcoholism will be found in CHAPTER II. The more specific details of medical and neuropsychiatric consequences and treatment will be found in CHAPTERS III and IV, and material on psychological and adjunctive medical treatments will be found in CHAPTERS V and VI respectively.

DEFINITION

Alcoholism is a chronic, progressive and addictive disease characterized by a craving for alcohol and its effect—a subjective state of well-being. The onset of the disease is based initially on a complicated psychological disturbance and facilitated by social and cultural factors. Once excessive drinking has begun in the psychologically susceptible individual, a series of additional processes ensue—nutritional deficiencies, addiction, involvement of various organ systems, and progressive psychological impairment. On the basis of these processes there follows further serious pathology of the organism at all levels of integration with the development of a multitude of characteristic complications—medical, neuropsychiatric, psychological, social and vocational. The natural course of the disease is usually a progressively downhill curve on which there may be superimposed exacerbations and remissions.

Alcoholism may also be defined in simple terms as drinking that brings about for the drinker or people around him serious problems in physical, mental, family, social or economic areas.

From the point of view of industry, a limited but practical definition of a problem drinker is: an individual whose repeated or continued over-indulgence interferes with the efficient performance of his work assignment.

ETIOLOGY

In the present state of our knowledge concerning the etiology of alcoholism, psychological factors appear to be the most significant. Many concepts from the psychological area concerning etiology are convincing both in the degree to which so much of the phenomenology of alcoholism is accounted for and from the application of theory to effective treatment procedures of various types. It is a universal observation that alcoholics have severe emotional conflicts, are immature and have difficulties in personal relations, all of which reflect themselves in maladaptation in the work and social areas. With careful study these defects are observed to be present in either obvious or occult form prior to the outbreak of the disease and are aggravated and added to following the onset of the disease.

The pre-morbid psychological defects of the alcoholic may be summed up under the headings of egocentricity, insufficient involvement with persons in the environment, and a pathologically immature and dependent relationship to these people. Alcohol is used by such individuals in an attempt to establish an equilibrium which for them is not feasible in the usual course of life pursuits and interests. (See CHAPTER III for details of the psychology of alcoholism.)

As for cultural differences, the high incidence of alcoholism among the Irish and the low incidence of alcoholism among the Chinese and Jews constitute impressive data. These differences are best viewed, however, as the result of historical and sociocultural differences rather than as the result of metabolic differences as claimed by some.

The occurrence of alcoholism on the basis of the causative factors of heredity and constitutional defects in the form of inborn metabolic or endocrine defects have been postulated and experimental and clinical evidence offered in support. However, though hereditary and constitutional factors must be borne in mind, their mode of operation and clinical importance have not as yet been convincingly demonstrated.

A consideration of hereditary factors in the etiology of alcoholism begins with the fact that alcoholism occurs with higher incidence in some families as compared with others. Jellinek [1] combined a number of studies and found that of a total of 4372 alcoholics 52 per cent had an alcoholic parent. The normal expectancy of alcoholism among children of alcoholics is approximately 25 per cent as compared with an expectancy of approximately 2 per cent for the general population.

While the facts themselves remain unquestioned, it is the explanation of these facts that lead to differences of opinion. There are some who use the above facts to substantiate the thesis that alcoholism is inherited. R. J. Williams[4] has offered a "genetotrophic" theory of alcoholism which suggests that certain individuals inherit metabolic patterns which result in nutritional deficiencies that give rise to a craving for alcohol. While Williams' hypotheses have not been generally confirmed, the theory remains a useful one for further research. In interpreting Jellinek's data a factor of greater weight than heridity appears to be that the children of alcoholics are exposed to the important etiological influence of disturbed alcoholic parents with the consequent occurrence of emotional disturbances in the children. As for the choice of alcoholism as a neurosis, the children of alcoholic parents have their parents as emotionally significant models for drinking. A striking example in reverse, emphasizing the importance of environmental parental influence in determining psychological attitudes towards drinking, is the not infrequent case of the teetotaler who has reacted against the alcoholic parent.

An important study is reported by Anne Roe.[2] A group of 36 children of alcoholic parents who had been separated from their parents were reared by non-alcoholic foster parents. At the time of the follow-up study report they had reached the age of 21 or over. A control group of children born of non-alcoholic parents but also raised in foster homes was used for comparison. As regards their adjustment there were no significant differences between the two groups, and there were as many seriously maladjusted individuals among the normal parentage group as there were among the alcoholic parentage group. It could not be said that the children of alcoholic parentage turned out as expected on the basis of any hypothesis of hereditary taint. None of the children of alcoholic parents became alcoholics and only three used alcohol regularly. Naturally it is difficult to know if some of these people will become alcoholics in the future; however, the fact that so few use alcohol now and that most of them have established adequate personal adjustment gives good reason to expect that few if any will become alcoholics.

Smith,[3] pursuing the problem of etiology from the point of view of endocrine disturbance, is of the opinion that alcoholism is essentially a metabolic disease. His studies have demonstrated deficiencies of the pituitary-adrenal-gonadal glands in a significant number of alcoholics. While it is unquestioned that in the course of alcoholism such endocrine defects do occur, it has generally been thought that these changes are secondary to excessive drinking rather than primary causes. Although no one has yet convincingly demonstrated that the alcoholic possesses a metabolic individuality which *predisposes* him to alcoholism, the hypotheses of Williams and Smith remain important and useful. It is hoped that the research going on at many medical centers will one day elicit a simple chemical cause of alcoholism and along with it a simple direct cure. At present, however, psychological factors appear to be the most convincing.

MEDICAL AND PERSONAL CONSEQUENCES

In addition to original etiology, one must consider a series of pathologies that come into play in the susceptible person once excessive drinking has begun:

1. Alcohol, through chemical, physiological and psychological mechanisms, relieves psychic and physical pain.

2. Tolerance for and consumption of alcohol increases. Abstinence results in a withdrawal syndrome for which more alcohol is taken. Meanwhile there develops a centering of interest on alcohol, a loss of interest in one's own physical, mental and social assets, and further loss of interest in family, friends and work. All of these constitute a picture of addiction qualitatively comparable, for example, to morphine addiction.

3. On the basis of the toxic effects of alcohol, produced in part by chemical mechanisms involving vitamin deficiencies due to impaired nutrition, tissue changes occur in various systems, especially the gastrointestinal and central nervous systems. Although in addition to psychic distress, physical pain may have been an important factor in the onset of alcoholism, the development of specific physical and neuropsychiatric syndromes aggravates pain and the vicious circle continues.

4. Most commonly, the alcoholic brings psychological defects to his drinking. These, too, are aggravated and further complicated by drinking, thus resulting in increased psychic pain.

On the basis of the original psychological predisposition and the above pathological mechanisms, a series of characteristic complications ensue. They may be grouped in the following categories: Medical, Neuropsychiatric, Psychological, Marital and Social, and Vocational.

Medical

A group of characteristic medical syndromes occur as complications of alcoholism: acute alcoholism, hangover, coma, gastritis, and hepatic disease are quite common. Cardiovascular disorders are rare. Skin manifestations are particularly common. (See CHAPTER III for detailed discussion.)

Neuropsychiatric

Various neuropsychiatric syndromes complicate alcoholism: peripheral neuropathy, delirium tremens, convulsive seizures, acute hallucinosis, alcoholic deterioration, and the alcoholic paranoid type are often seen. Wernicke's syndrome, nicotinic acid deficiency encephalopathy, and Korsakoff's psychosis are not commonly seen. Only a few cases of Marchiafava's disease have been reported. Cases of pathologic intoxication are seen mostly in psychiatric prison wards. (See CHAPTER IV for detailed discussions.)

Psychological

The psychological defects of the alcoholic are the product of defects present prior to drinking and regression due to the drinking itself. In addition, there are the psychological defects consequent to cerebral organic changes and metabolic derangements. In cases where the disease process is well established, one may observe loss of a sense of ethics, varying with periods of extreme guilt and remorse; impairment of the ability to distinguish between a subjective feeling or thought and reality; loss of involvement with usual social interests such as people, work and hobbies. There may be the non-acceptance of feelings and thoughts as one's own and the ascribing of them to others. There may be a retreat to a rich fantasy life or direct engaging in various sexual and aggressive drives. (See CHAPTER IV.)

Marital and Social

In the marital and social areas one sees typical changes complicating alcoholism. They eventuate from the psychological and organic changes already mentioned. There are the usual features of ignoring the needs of the family, family fights and destructive behavior, separation, divorce, loss of friends, and debt.

Work

In the work area one also sees features which occur in a strikingly consistent fashion: inefficiency at work, loss of time, fights with supervisors stemming from the erroneous feeling of being "picked on" in an unfair way, the quitting of and loss of jobs.

DIAGNOSIS

The diagnosis of alcoholism in far-advanced cases presents little difficulty. In cases of moderate severity, the diagnosis rests on the history obtained from the patient and outside sources, an evaluation of the patient's drinking habits, his behavior while drinking, his home, work and personal relations, and physical and laboratory examinations. From the psychological point of view, the factors that would point to the diagnosis of alcoholism would be (in addition to all of the above): the special features of a preoccupation with alcohol and a compulsion to drink; the centering of interests on the obtaining and using of alcohol together with a deterioration of the patient's relations with people at home, at work and socially.

There are, however, many instances of doubtful cases where it is not readily determinable that the diagnosis of alcoholism should be made. From a clinical point of view, a useful approach is to translate the term "alcoholism" into "problem drinking." If it is determined that the individual has problems at work, at home or in the physical or neuropsychiatric spheres related to drinking, it may be stated that he has a drinking problem and in any event should have treatment. When presented with the word "alcoholism" the alcoholic will often only deny it more vigorously. The term "problem drinking" is more acceptable to him. To the alcoholic the latter term implies only that in relation to drinking there are various problems, and he finds it easier to agree to this and to pursue the exploration with the physician.

PROGNOSIS

The prognosis in cases of alcoholism may be discussed in terms of *curability, recurrence,* and *arrest.*

Cure, in the sense of the ability to again drink socially, once the disease has become well-established, is practically unknown. Recurrence of all the manifestations of alcoholism is common if drinking recurs even after total abstinence for as long a period as twenty years.

As for spontaneous arrest of the disease without formal treatment of some kind, it is difficult to know what the statistical incidence is, but it certainly does occur in many cases. With treatment measured in terms of total abstinence, according to most reports, arrestability appears to be possible in approximately 50 per cent of cases. The percentage of arrested cases in any particular setting depends on factors such as the selection of cases, the treatment methods used, and the interest and skill of the therapist. In some situations 60 per cent and higher significant arrests can be obtained in relation to specially favorable circumstances. (See CHAPTERS VII and VIII.)

As for the possibility of arrest in the individual case, this seems to rest primarily on the degree of motivation present or potentially present in the patient. If the alcoholic is not motivated to use assistance properly, he cannot be helped. (See CHAPTER V under Motivation.)

TREATMENT

As indicated previously, the alcoholic experiences impairment on many levels. All of these defects require treatment. Although there are several different ways of treating alcoholics (medical, psychiatric, Alcoholics Anonymous) there is only one goal—total abstinence. Furthermore, the achievement of abstinence will in a remarkable and rapid fashion affect marked improvement in most or all of the complications of drinking.

It is a matter of clinical judgment as to which form of treatment is best suited for a particular patient. In some instances best results can be obtained through Alcoholics Anonymous, in others a psychiatric approach is indicated. There are some alcoholic patients who cannot accept, at least initially, the idea of psychiatric treatment or Alcoholics Anonymous. Such patients may be treated by the general physician. In the treatment of alcoholics, it is most important that one have the patient's cooperation and it is usually best to respect the patient's strong convictions concerning the choice in type of treatment. Obviously this would not apply, for example, to the mentally disturbed and destructive patient who voices objections to hospitalization. Regarding the results of various approaches to the treatment of alcoholics, there is no data to indicate that one approach achieves distinctly better therapeutic results than another. Each has its usefulness in different types of problems. (See following CHAPTERS for details of treatment.)

REFERENCES

1. JELLINEK, E. M.: Quoted in: Clinebel, H. J., Understanding and Counseling the Alcoholic. New York, Abingdon Press, 1956, p. 42.
2. ROE, A.: Children of alcoholic parents raised in foster homes. Alcohol, Science and Society. Quart. J. Stud. Alcohol 1945.
3. SMITH, J. J.: A medical approach to problem drinking. Quart. J. Stud. Alcohol 10: 251–257, 1949.
4. WILLIAMS, R. J.: The etiology of alcoholism. Quart. J. Stud. on Alcohol 7: 567–587, 1947.

II   *Management of the Medical Complications of Alcoholism* *

THE COURSE of alcoholism and the management of the alcoholic are complicated by a number of medical conditions directly or indirectly brought about by excessive drinking. Several organ systems may be simultaneously involved by these processes.

In addition to the medical states commonly associated with alcoholism, the alcoholic is somewhat more prone to infections, head injuries and other traumata than is the non-alcoholic. As a consequence, the alcoholic frequently shows evidence of multiple illnesses against which, because of general debility, he is often unable to muster adequate defense.

The importance of a thorough medical history and careful physical, neurologic and laboratory examinations is self evident.

ACUTE ALCOHOLISM

The acute alcoholic state † may be defined as a period of uncontrolled drinking that interferes with a person's ability to function effectively. The duration is often determined only by the patient's ability to continue to drink, and this may vary widely in different persons.

Acute alcoholic intoxication is seen both in chronic drinkers and as an isolated condition in individuals who have overestimated their capacity for intoxicants. The condition is due to the depression of the higher (and inhibitory) cerebral centers, which is one of the physiological effects of alcohol. The behavior pattern during acute alcoholism depends upon the degree of cerebral depression and the basic personality traits of the individual concerned.

Many hold that it is useless to attempt to treat anyone during the acute alcoholic state unless the phase has run its course and the patient himself is desirous of treatment. This may be generally true, but not infrequently the physician may be able to convince a patient to accept treatment despite considerable reservation on the patient's part. If the therapy administered can successfully interrupt the drinking and ease the difficult postalcoholic period, as many of the newer methods can,

* The material in this chapter was revised by Daniel J. Feldman, M.D., and Sidney S. Greenberg, M.D.

† Additional information on this subject is available.[8-10, 17, 19, 23-25, 27]

then such unnecessary suffering is eliminated and the possibility of a serious tragedy may be avoided.

The specific management of the acute alcoholic state may be conveniently considered in the following areas:

Correction of physical and physiological abnormalities

Correction of abnormalities should include consideration of fluid balance, correction of salt and nutritional deficiencies when they exist, and diagnosis and correction of existing diseases. Most patients who have been drinking in an uncontrolled fashion for any length of time have sustained some degree of dehydration. This state should be recognized and corrected. In mild cases in which the patient is cooperative, the oral administration of whatever fluids the patient prefers is sufficient. In view of recent concepts that implicate adrenal hypofunction in the acute alcoholic state, the use of salt in the treatment of this condition has often been made a routine procedure. When possible, a patient may take it by mouth. The intravenous use of isotonic sodium chloride solution is, of course, always available.

The use of vitamins, particularly the B group and vitamin C, is warranted since all other foods are often abandoned for alcohol and since a certain degree of acute avitaminosis can be presumed present after a drinking bout of more than a few days. In addition, the effect of vitamins of the B group on the liver, and of vitamin C on the adrenal gland, is beneficial. Vitamins can be administered orally or intravenously. Large doses of vitamin B and at least 0.5 to 1 Gm. of vitamin C should be given daily for the first two or three days.

Management of symptoms associated with acute alcoholic intoxication and the immediate post-alcoholic state

Symptoms such as marked hyperexcitability, restlessness, and nausea or vomiting may be features of acute intoxication, and their control is an important part of the management of the patient.

The use of chlorpromazine (Thorazine), promazine (Sparine) and meprobamate greatly facilitates the management of these symptoms. Their use decreases the possibility of barbiturate or other habituation—always a hazard in the alcoholic patient—by making excessive use of sedatives unnecessary. Nausea and vomiting associated with the acute state are markedly diminished and adequate oral feeding can usually be instituted fairly promptly. Intravenous alimentation and hydration are often entirely unnecessary. The incidence of delirium tremens as a complication of acute intoxication seems to be diminished through the preventive effect of these newer medications.

The profound tranquillizing effect of chlorpromazine (Thorazine) can so depress the psychomotor hyperactivity that the patient is scarcely aware of its existence. The anti-emetic properties of the drug give it further value when nausea, vomiting and retching are prominent symptoms.

At the onset of treatment chlorpromazine should be given in sufficiently large doses to insure adequate depression of activity and sleep, if possible: the oral or parenteral route may be used depending on the patient's condition. When a patient is in coma or stupor when first seen, chlorpromazine should be withheld until sufficient activity develops to warrant its use. The size of the initial dose will depend on the condition of the individual patient, the degree of psychomotor hyperactivity being the most important consideration. Doses of 75 to 100 mg. are usually adequate although on occasion more may be necessary. Following the initial dose, subsequent therapy will depend on the needs of the individual being treated. Such factors as subjective feelings of anxiety, tremor and jitteriness will influence the dosage. Patients should be kept on treatment for four to seven days. The amount of the drug is reduced as the patient improves, and usually 25 mg. three or four times daily is sufficient to maintain a state of tranquillity. On such a regimen the patient is usually cooperative and relaxed. It should be mentioned that because of the hypotensive effect of chlorpromazine some patients may develop severe postural hypotension particularly during the first few days of therapy. Those concerned with taking care of the patient should be warned of the possibility.

Promazine (Sparine) has recently been used in the treatment of acute alcoholism. The indications for its use are identical with those of chlorpromazine. An initial dose of 20 to 100 mg. seems adequate and this dosage is repeated every four to six hours as the condition of the patient warrants. The drug may be given parenterally when the patient is unable to take it orally. If anything, promazine seems more effective than chlorpromazine in controlling psychomotor hyperactivity and other symptoms of the acute and post-withdrawal phases. The hypotension and compensatory tachycardia are less pronounced, and gastric symptoms are efficiently controlled. The presence of severe liver disease seems to offer no contraindication.

Meprobamate (Miltown, Equanil) in doses of 400 to 600 mg. three to six times daily may be used in the management of milder cases of acute intoxication, but is not as effective as chlorpromazine or promazine in moderate or severe cases. It has proven of value in the management of symptoms associated with the immediate post-alcoholic state when they have abated to a point no longer requiring the more potent ataractics.

With the availability of ataractics the extensive use of adrenal corticosteroids in the management of acute alcoholism has greatly decreased. At this time they are usually reserved for these patients in whom ataractics are either ineffective or poorly tolerated. Twenty-five mg. of corticotropin (ACTH) in an infusion may be administered. Such an infusion should take from six to eight hours to administer. Oral or parenteral administration of adrenal corticosteroids (cortisone 25 to 50 mg. every six to eight hours, prednisolone 5 to 10 mg. every six to eight hours, prednisone 5 to 10 mg. every six to eight hours) have proved quite effective. If significant cardiac or renal disease is present, the use of ataractics is probably safer.

ALCOHOLIC COMA

Alcoholic coma is a medical emergency calling for quick, vigorous and definitive treatment. Coma results when sufficient alcohol has been ingested to cause profound depression of the central nervous system. It is analagous to deep anesthetic narcosis, the physiological mechanism of both phenomena being identical. If sufficiently severe, depression of the respiratory center and death can result. Blood alcohol levels in patients suffering from alcoholic coma are in the range of 360 to 480 mg. per cent (Gettler).

A correct diagnosis requires the elimination of other causes of coma. A good history, preferably from a close friend or relative, is a valuable aid. Thorough laboratory study is sometimes necessary before a correct diagnosis can be achieved. Blood sugar and blood alcohol studies are important. Careful search for signs of head traumata must be made; alcoholics frequently incur these injuries, and the smell of alcohol on a patient's breath may lead to the incorrect diagnosis of alcoholic coma where actually a serious head injury exists. When the possibility of a central nervous system infection is present, spinal puncture and bacteriologic and cytologic studies of the cerebrospinal fluid should be made.

When the diagnosis is that of alcoholic coma, gastric aspiration should be performed promptly. Caution should be exercised to prevent aspiration of the gastric contents with the subsequent development of pneumonia. Lowering the head during this procedure will assist in preventing this complication. If much secretion is found in the pharyngotrachael region, the use of an intratracheal airway will prevent obstruction. The patient should be kept warm and signs of peripheral vascular collapse anticipated. Immediate measures to combat shock are imperative, and stimulants are usually indicated. Intramuscular caffeine-sodium benzoate in doses of 10 to 15 grains (0.7 to 1.0 Gm.), together with ephedrine sulfate given intramuscularly in doses of 0.5 grains (0.3 Gm.) can be effective in awakening the patient. These medications may be administered every two hours if necessary. When the coma is very deep (as indicated by neuropsychiatric signs and blood alcohol levels) picrotoxin may be indicated. Generally one cc. of a 1:1000 solution is injected intraveneously per minute until the pupillary and corneal reflexes return, and care must be exercised to avoid the development of convulsions.[4] Intraveneous metrazol in doses of 5 cc. of a 10 per cent solution is reported as being effective in both comatose and excited patients.[5] Intravenous methamphetamine (Desoxyephedrine) or d-amphetamine (Dexidrene) in doses of 10 to 30 mg. every 30 to 60 minutes can be used when patient is responding to small doses of picrotoxin until some degree of consciousness has returned. When the coma is very severe and the respiration slow and shallow (blood alcohol concentrations near the fatal level of 500 mg. per cent), the use of carbon dioxide (5 to 10 per cent) and oxygen (to 95 per cent) by inhalation is valuable and serves as a respiratory stimulant.

GASTRITIS *

Both acute and chronic gastritis occur with sufficient frequency in the course of alcoholism to be considered a complication of the disease. The most common cause of acute gastritis is overindulgence in alcohol with its concomitant irritant effect on the mucosa. Relatively little is known of the pathology of this condition; such information as is available has been gained through the use of the gastroscope, and in those rare cases in which it is possible to observe the gastric mucosa through a fistulous opening. Such gastroscopic and direct studies indicate that

* Additional information on this subject is available.[3, 4, 7, 12, 18, 28]

frequently there is no correlation between the degree of change observed pathologically and the clinical symptoms. The lesion of acute gastritis usually clears completely with treatment, but occasionally it passes into a chronic form without returning to normal.

Varying degrees of epigastric burning and distress, nausea, anorexia, vomiting and diarrhea are the chief complaints. Prostration and extreme weakness can result. An acute fulminating form is observed after a prolonged alcoholic debauch, when the picture is comparable to that of an acute abdominal catastrophe, and the differential diagnosis from an acute condition calling for surgical intervention is frequently difficult.

In mild cases withholding all oral intake for 12 to 24 hours followed by liquid, soft and bland diets, is usually adequate treatment. In more severe cases sedation may be necessary. When nausea and vomiting are severe, the use of chlorpromazine, promazine or compazine will prove quite helpful. Fluid and electrolyte balances are maintained by intravenous fluids when necessary. With improvement, the gradual use of liquid, soft and bland diets is instituted. The response to treatment is usually prompt and satisfactory.

Although chronic gastritis is associated with many conditions and frequently is idiopathic, the incidence in alcoholics is sufficiently great to warrant its inclusion as a complication of alcoholism. In a small percentage of alcoholics, chronic gastritis may be the direct aftermath of acute gastritis. Frequent repeated attacks of acute gastritis, not necessarily accompanied by clinical manifestations, probably precede the development of a chronic gastritis. The factors of avitaminosis and malnutrition may play a part. It is important to note that there is a great difference in the susceptibility of the gastric mucosa in different individuals.

Basically, two types of chronic gastritis are noted: the atrophic and the hypertrophic. These are essentially two distinct diseases, unrelated to each other. The atrophic type is the form commonly associated with alcoholism. This condition may vary from a superficial involvement of the mucosa to complete atrophy, with smoothing out of the folds and degeneration of the secreting parenchyma; gastric acidity tends to be low or absent.

The symptoms of chronic atrophic gastritis are exceedingly variable and are not correlated with the pathological change. The digestive complaints are, as a rule, periodic in occurrence. Most commonly they consist of dull epigastric pain or discomfort without radiation and associated anorexia or nausea. The symptoms usually occur postprandially; these is no night pain. The patient does not obtain relief from either food or alkali. General symptoms of marked fatigue and weakness are common although there is some question as to whether these symptoms are due to the gastritis itself. Bleeding is extremely rare.

Anemia is frequently of the hypochromic microcytic type. The mechanism of its production is not certain. Many etiologic factors seem to be involved, among them vitamin deficiency and gastrointestinal dysfunction with poor iron absorption. The anemia may improve as the gastritis improves without specific anti-anemic therapy. In a small number of patients a hyperchromic macrocytic anemia is found.

Complete abstinence from alcohol is essential in the treatment. Elimination of other gastrointestinal irritants such as drugs (salycilates, iodides), drastic cathartics, excessive tea or coffee, very hot or cold liquids, and excessive smoking is indicated. Rest immediately before and after meals is of value and in severe cases a period of complete bed rest may be necessary. The diet should be essentially bland and taken in small and frequent feedings. Additional vitamins, especially vitamins B and C, are desirable because they are apt to be present in inadequate amounts, and also because the diet may be deficient in them (due to the paucity of fruits and vegetables). Gastric lavage is rarely necessary but may be indicated in severe cases when there is much desquamation and exudation. Its use in the early morning hours is recommended. The initial lavage should be carried out with a weak solution of hydrogen peroxide followed by saline until the returning fluid becomes clear. Dilute HCl can be tried in cases of atrophic gastritis with achlorhydria. It will sometimes alleviate the gastric symptoms and is best given immediately before meals. Antacids and antispasmodics are not of much use in the treatment of the atrophic form of chronic gastritis. Hypochromic anemias should be treated with iron and vitamin therapy, particularly vitamin B complex. Adequate amounts of pyridoxine must be administered. Certain cases refractory to this treatment may require additional therapy in the form of vitamin B_{12} or liver extracts.

HEPATIC DISEASE *

The liver disease commonly associated with alcoholism is diffuse hepatic fibrosis-portal cirrhosis of the Laennec type. There is no incon-

* Additional information on this subject is available.[1, 2, 5, 6, 13-16, 20-22]

trovertible evidence which establishes any direct etiologic relationship between alcohol and this condition, but its association with alcoholism must be considered as more than merely casual. At present the role of alcohol in the development of portal cirrhosis can be considered only contributory. Experimental and clinical evidence point to nutritional changes as the fundamental abnormality, and these changes consist primarily of deficiencies in protein and vitamins. Fatty infiltration of the liver seems to be associated with the development of cirrhosis, and is held by some investigators to be a precursor of it. Among the physical signs commonly associated with portal cirrhosis, any or all of the following may be present: hepatomegaly, splenomegaly, jaundice, abdominal caput, ascites, edema, spider angiomata, loss of hair, and esophageal varices. Symptoms of liver dysfunction are very often absent despite clear-cut objective evidence of the existence of cirrhosis.

The various signs and symptoms are related to abnormalities of the several functions of the liver and are best considered from that point of view. When the excretory function is impaired, the most outstanding finding is the elevation of the serum bilirubin and ultimately the development of clinical jaundice. The cholesterol and alkaline phosphatase level of the blood will also be elevated when the jaundice is due to obstruction of the portal bile passages. These findings are usually late developments in the course of portal cirrhosis.

Obstruction of the portal system occurs when fibrosis has developed sufficiently to interfere with the intrahepatic circulation. In such cases, portal hypertension has been demonstrated by direct measurements of the pressure in the portal system. Splenomegaly and the development of collateral circulation (esophageal, hemmorhoidal, and periumbilical) have been attributed to portal hypertension. The grave complication of bleeding varices of the esophagus arises from the development of a collateral circulation in that area.

Portal hypertension plays a part in the development of ascites and possibly edema, but the mechanism is not clear-cut. Ascites, and particularly edema, may be correlated with changes in the blood proteins, especially with a decrease of albumin. The mechanism of the production of ascites and edema is a complicated one; such factors as hypoproteinemia, high capillary pressure due to portal hypertension, increased capillary permeability, and failure of adequate salt and water excretion may all play a part.

Pain is not a common symptom in portal cirrhosis; however, a sense of fullness or pressure due to an enlarged liver may be present. When they are marked, nausea and vomiting can be aggravating symptoms. General complaints are of fatigue, weakness, and weight loss.

The anemias associated with portal cirrhosis are poorly understood. If microcytic hypochromic anemia is present, it is apt to respond slowly to iron but may improve spontaneously with the amelioration of the liver disease. When splenomegaly is present, the anemia may be due to hypersplenism. The association of macrocytic anemias and portal cirrhosis is well-known, although exact nature and cause are not clear. Wintrobe feels that macrocytic anemia is probably due to the inability of the liver to store the hematopoietic principle. Parenteral liver extract or vitamin B_{12} may or may not correct this type of anemia—the response to therapy being frequently poor.

In the presence of advanced disease, a picture of terminal liver failure is sometimes seen. General weakness and asthenia are marked. Clouded sensorium, mental changes, and varying abnormal neurological signs are observed. Ultimately, coma supervenes. Jaundice may be intense and progressive, and bleeding in various portions of the body occurs. Biochemical tests reveal a profound disturbance of hepatic function. The vast majority of patients who arrive at this state succumb, but recovery occasionally occurs.

The most accurate and objective evaluation of liver function can be obtained by the use of specially designed tests. However, since any single test can measure but one specific function, it is well to utilize a battery of several in order to secure an over-all picture of the functional state. Such tests as the serum bilirubin level, icteric index, and bromsulfalein excretion measure the excretory function of the liver. The urinary urobilinogen is a delicate and early measure of dysfunction and will be abnormal in the early nutritional phase of liver disease. Serum protein levels and the albumin and globulin ratio, the thymol turbidity test, cephalin flocculation, cholesterol level, and the degree of esterification all measure the parenchymal function of the liver. Prothrombin studies may be regarded as a test of liver function. The best *single* test is the bromsulphalein excretion.

Puncture biopsy of the liver is an exceedingly helpful tool for the study of liver disease although no consistent correlation can be found between the cirrhotic change noted in the biopsy specimen and the clinical state of the patient. The progress or remission of the pathologic process can be followed, and definite and specific diagnosis is possible through its use.

The brilliant work of Patek, and Patek and Post, provides the basis for the general treatment of portal cirrhosis, which may be summarized as follows: All alcohol should be eschewed. A nutritious diet high in proteins, vitamins, and carbohydrates and of moderate fat content, is remarkably effective. Although the importance of an absent or low fat content has been stressed in the past, it has been amply demonstrated that a moderate fat content does not injure the patient but on the contrary greatly improves his appetite and well-being when it is combined with a high protein content. To this diet are added large amounts of supplemental vitamins, particularly of the B complex; vitamin A should be given because the diseased liver is unable to store this substance in the form of carotene. These are given as vitamin concentrates or in the form of brewer's yeast. There is not much evidence favoring the use of choline or methionine at this stage of the disease; their value in the fatty liver is still open to question. Adequate rest should be insured. Added to this regimen are certain specific measures for the various complications which may be present. Ascites is treated by abdominal paracentesis, and this is performed as often as may be necessary for the comfort of the patient. There is not much to be gained from the use of mercurial diuretics. However, a low sodium diet may be of some advantage.

Bleeding esophageal varices—when they endanger life—must be approached surgically through vascular shunting operations.

The macrocytic anemia which accompanies portal cirrhosis is treated with iron and blood transfusion when necessary. When the existence of hypersplenism is suspected and the anemia is refractory and dangerous, splenectomy may be necessary.

CARDIOVASCULAR DISORDERS *

Alcoholic patients are liable to all the usual cardiovascular diseases noted in medical practice. The cardiac symptoms of alcoholics are rarely due to alcoholism or its related nutritional deficiencies. However, existing heart disease can be aggravated by the abnormal living habits so commonly noted in this group of patients. The treatment follows the same rules as does that of heart disease in general. Increased psychomotor activity, such as occurs in delirium tremens or in certain forms of

* Additional information on this subject is available.[11, 29-31]

acute alcoholism, can precipitate the development of heart failure in patients with compensated heart disease. It is probable that failure may be produced in patients with markedly increased psychomotor activity even when there is no pre-existing evidence of heart disease. This will occur chiefly in malnourished and debilitated patients. There is no clear-cut evidence of any direct effect of alcohol on the myocardium itself.

The type of heart disease specifically associated with chronic alcoholism is that due to thiamine deficiency. Although relatively rare in its pure form, even among alcoholics, it may be a complicating feature in other forms of heart disease and confuse the patient's response to therapy. The symptoms, when they are marked, are similar to other forms of heart disease. The physical findings on the whole are also not characteristic. There is some tendency toward the development of peripheral vascular collapse and shock states which, when present, may help in making a specific diagnosis. The findings of "pistol shot" murmurs over the femoral artery and wide pulse pressures are also helpful. The diagnosis for the most part depends on the presence of other evidence of thiamine deficiency. Evidence of polyneuritis, skin manifestations of avitaminosis, glossitis, etc. are all useful points. A history of a deficient diet for three months or more is suggestive of the diagnosis. The response of the cardiovascular signs and symptoms to treatment with thiamine chloride is probably the best criterion.

Vitamin C deficiency can be mentioned as a possible cause of cardiovascular disease. Hemorrhage into the heart and pericardium has been described experimentally, and there is a possibility that degeneration of the heart muscle itself may occur.

The treatment of vitamin deficiency in heart disease consists primarily in the administration of adequate amounts of thiamine chloride. Doses of 100 mg. daily by subcutaneous injection are recommended. An adequate protein intake necessary for the proper utilization of thiamine must be insured. Rest in bed is extremely important. When the disease is of short duration and not advanced, the response to specific therapy may be striking. Occasionally, in chronic forms, the myocardial changes are irreversible. Salt restriction should be utilized and other vitamin deficiencies corrected.

There is some question as to the advisability of administering mercurial diuretics and digitalis. They can be used as in other cases of congestive heart failure, but it should be remembered that their effect will be only slight as long as the thiamine deficiency remains uncorrected.

SKIN MANIFESTATIONS

The skin lesions which are peculiar to alcoholics are primarily allergic manifestations and the dermatologic lesions of avitaminosis. Allergic manifestations may be due to sensitization to such specific substances as the proteins of barley, malt, yeast and rye. A non-specific alcoholic effect occurs due to the increased permeability of the gastrointestinal barrier following the ingestion of alcohol. Under such circumstances, ingested food allergens are absorbed into the circulation in sufficiently high concentration to cause manifestations of sensitivity in individuals who, under ordinary circumstances, have a high enough gastrointestinal threshhold to avoid symptoms even though they are sensitive to the food in question.

Skin lesions characteristic of the vitamin deficiencies are most commonly seen in alcoholic patients. Thiamine chloride, riboflavin, nicotinic acid, and vitamin A and C deficiencies must be considered in a diagnosis of dermatologic lesions in alcoholics. Multiple vitamin deficiencies must always be kept in mind.

Rosacea with rhinophyma is commonly associated with chronic alcoholism; in severe cases, surgical treatment of the nasal lesion must be undertaken.

REFERENCES

1. BATEMAN, J. C., SHORR, H. M., AND ELGVIN, T. J.: Hypervolemic anemia in cirrhosis. J. Clin. Invest. *28:* 539, 1949.
2. BEST, C. H., AND LUCAS, C. C.: Vitamins and Hormones. Vol. 1. New York, Academic Press, 1943.
3. BOCKUS, H. L., BANK, J., AND WILLARD, J. H.: Achlorhydria with a review of 210 cases in patients with gastrointestinal complaints. Am. J. Med. Sc. *184:* 185, 1932.
4. ——: Gastroenterology. Vol. I. Philadelphia, W. B. Saunders & Co., 1943.
5. CONNOR, C. L.: Fatty infiltration of the liver and the development of cirrhosis in diabetes and chronic alcoholism. Am. J. Path. *14:* 347, 1938.
6. ——: Etiology and pathogenesis of alcoholic cirrhosis of liver. J.A.M.A. *112:* 387, 1939.
7. FABER, KNUD H.: Gastritis and Its Consequences. Oxford Medical Publication, London, 1935.
8. FELDMAN, D. J., AND ZUCKER, H. D.: Present day medical management of alcoholism. J.A.M.A. *153:* 895, 1953.
9. ——: Treatment of chronic alcoholism: a survey of current methods. Ann. Int. Med. *44:* 78, 1956.
10. ——: Drug therapy of chronic alcoholism. Med. Clin. N. A. *41:* 381, 1957.

11. FRIEDBERG, C. K.: Diseases of the Heart, ed. 2. Philadelphia, W. B. Saunders & Co., 1956.
12. GRAY, S., AND SCHINDLER, R.: Gastric mucosa of chronic alcoholic addicts: gastroscopic study. J.A.M.A. *117*: 1005, 1941.
13. HIMSWORTH, H. P.: The Liver and Its Diseases. Cambridge, Harvard University Press, 1947.
14. ——, AND GLYNN, L. E.: Massive hepatic necrosis and diffuse hepatic fibrosis. Clin. Sci. *5*: 93, 1945.
15. JARROLD, T., AND VILTER, R. W.: Hematologic observations in patients with chronic hepatic insufficiency. J. Clin. Invest. *28*: 286, 1949.
16. HOFFBAUER, F. W.: Liver. Am. Rev. Phys. *11*: 83, 1949.
17. MCALLISTER, R. G.: Use of adrenal cortical hormone in alcoholism: report of 100 consecutive cases. Virginia Med. *79*: 70, 1952.
18. MULROONEY, R. E.: Cytology of gastric contents in reference to gastritis. Proc. Staff Meet., Mayo Clin. *15*: 81, 1940.
19. NICHOLSON, W. M., AND TAYLOR, H. M.: The effect of alcohol on the water and electrolyte balance in man. J. Clin. Invest. *17*: 279, 1938.
20. PATEK, A. J., JR., AND POST, J.: Treatment of cirrhosis of the liver by a nutritious diet and supplements rich in vitamin B complex. J. Clin. Invest. *20*: 481, 1941.
21. —— et al.: Dietary treatment of cirrhosis of liver: results in 124 patients observed during 10 year period. J.A.M.A. *138*: 543, 1948.
22. POST, J., AND ROSE, J. V.: Clinical, functional and histologic studies in Laennec's cirrhosis of liver. Am. J. Med. *8*: 300, 1950.
23. SHERFEY, M. J., AND DIETHELM, O.: Evaluation of drugs in treatment of alcoholism. A. Research. Nerv. & Mental Dis. Proc. *31*: 287, 1953.
24. SMITH, J. J.: Endocrine basis and hormone therapy of alcoholism. New York J. Med. *50*: 1704, 1950.
25. ——: Treatment of acute alcoholic states with ACTH and adreno-cortical hormones. Quart. J. Stud. Alcohol *11*: 190, 1950.
26. THIMANN, J., AND GAUTHIER, J. W.: Miltown as a tranquilizer in the treatment of alcohol addicts. Quart. J. Stud. Alcohol *17*: 19, 1956.
27. TINTERA, J. W., AND LOVELL, H. W.: Endocrine treatment of alcoholism. Geriatrics *4*: 274, 1949.
28. TUMEN, H. J., AND LIEBERTHAL, M. M.: Chronic gastritis: Review of its present status. New Internat. Clin. *(II)* 2: 263, 1941.
29. WEISS, S., AND WILKINS, R. W.: Nature of cardiovascular disturbances in nutritional deficiency states (beriberi). Am. Int. Med. *11*: 104, 1937.
30. ——: Occidental beriberi with cardiovascular manifestations: its relation to thiamin deficiency. J.A.M.A. *115*: 832, 1940.
31. WHITE, P. D.: Heart Disease, ed. 4. New York, Macmillan Co., 1951.

III *Management of Neuropsychiatric Complications of Alcoholism*

IN THE course of alcoholism one or more neuropsychiatric syndromes may occur in the same individual. One of the determining factors that appears to underlie these syndromes is the improper diet that usually accompanies alcoholism which contributes to an impaired metabolism. This is especially true in relation to inadequate intake or absorption of B vitamins, especially thiamine and niacin. These are important in basic enzyme functions. Additional factors are: the direct toxic effects of alcohol and subsequent impairment of biochemical (carbohydrate) and physiological (oxidation) processes.

Various portions of the nervous system may also be predominantly involved—peripheral nerves, spinal cord, nerve roots, cortex or midbrain. In addition underlying personality features may be revealed giving rise to a whole series of typical syndromes.

PERIPHERAL NEUROPATHY

Peripheral neuropathy in alcoholics is usually bilateral and symmetrical and characteristically involves first (and predominantly) the lower extremities. The onset of symptoms is usually slow but occasionally paralysis develops rapidly. The early symptoms are leg pains, paresthesias of hands and feet, and weakness of the muscles of the lower extremities. The cranial nerves are involved only in severe cases and in Wernicke's syndrome (see below.) Occasionally these may be associated with myelopathy or radiculopathy. Dryness, swelling, or pigmentation of the skin on the back of the wrists and hands and other evidences of vitamin deficiency are often present. The weakness of the muscles is greatest in the distal part of the extremity. Vibratory sense is impaired. The muscles, especially the calf muscles, are painful to pressure, and even the pressure of a bed cover may be unbearable. The ankle and knee jerks usually are lost as may also be the deep reflexes of the arm. There is a characteristic "after-burning" effect following stimulation of the soles of the feet. Occasionally the spinal fluid shows an increase in protein. Laboratory data are otherwise usually within normal limits. The course of the disease is usually prolonged, and it is ordinarily months before the patient is able to get out of bed—often a matter of six months to a year before he is able to walk. In addition, permanent disability of varying degree may remain. The relationship of peripheral neuropathy to thiamine deficiency has been clearly established.

In the treatment of the acute symptoms, immediate bed rest is important. When excessive tenderness of the muscles has disappeared, passive movements of the joints through their full range of motion should be instituted to prevent disabling contractures from developing. Plaster shells, bivalved so that they can be taken off for physiotherapy, may be applied to the legs and feet to maintain their proper position, and cock-up splints are often used for the wrists when wrist-drop is present. It is particularly important that these latter measures be used during the night. A well-rounded diet high in calories and vitamins should be administered, and polyvitamin supplements should be given. In addition, high doses (100 to 500 mg. per day) of thiamine chloride should be used for a long period of time.

WERNICKE'S SYNDROME [10]

Wernicke's syndrome is characterized by clouding of the consciousness and varying degress of ophthalmoplegia and ataxia. The syndrome, as originally described by Wernicke,[9] is probably a combination of severe nutritional deficiencies affecting the nervous system, and all its manifestations need not necessarily be present in any one case.[10] Delirium, with its marked increase in psychomotor activity and hence total metabolism, usually precedes the development of this syndrome. In such patients the early administration of thiamine will prevent the development of ophthalmoplegia (see under Delirium Tremens). In addition to nicotinic acid (500 to 1000 mg. per day orally for three to seven days), total vitamin B complex, and a nutritious diet, thiamine should be administered (50 to 100 mg. parenterally for two to seven days). The oculomotor palsies respond exceptionally well to thiamine. Other deficiency syndromes (pellagra, encephalopathy due to nicotinic acid deficiency, and riboflavin deficiency) can and do superimpose themselves on the more usual picture of Wernicke's syndrome and these require specific treatment.

NICOTINIC ACID DEFICIENCY ENCEPHALOPATHY

This is a term used by Jolliffe et al.[3] to designate a syndrome characterized by sucking and grasping reflexes, changing cogwheel rigidities of the extremities, and progressive clouding of the consciousness. Mortality is markedly reduced and signs and symptoms are improved by treatment with nicotinic acid (500 to 1000 mg. per day orally for three to seven days) or nicotinic acid amide (100 to 200 mg. per day parenterally for three to seven days). In addition, thiamine and the entire B complex should be given. These patients show residual memory defects.

MARCHIAFAVA'S DISEASE [4]

Marchiafava's disease is a primary progressive degeneration of the corpus callosum. The demyelenization begins at first in small areas, possibly around the vessels, then coalesces and affects mainly the genu and anterior part, but does not spare the rest. It has been described so far only in Italian males who had a long history of alcoholism. The syndrome occurs after middle age and is characterized essentially by progressive intellectual and emotional deterioration and the occurrence of epileptiform seizures. The condition is persistent and is diagnosed only at necropsy.

PATHOLOGIC INTOXICATION [2]

Pathologic intoxication is an acute reaction to even small amounts of alcohol and occurs in psychopathic, hysterical or epileptoid individuals. The outstanding characteristics of the pathologic reaction to alcohol are blind rage and confusion, with complete amnesia for the condition. It is not necessarily a manifestation of chronic alcoholism. Occasionally the reaction manifests itself as an ecstatic state rather than rage. The reaction may last from a few minutes to a few hours, and crimes of violence may be attempted.

DELIRIUM TREMENS [2]

Delirium tremens usually occurs in habitually severe and chronic alcoholics. It frequently follows injuries, operations, and acute infections. On physical examination, the conjunctivae and face are ordinarily found to be congested. The pupils are dilated and often react slowly. There is a coarse tremor of the extended fingers, tongue and muscles of the lips and face. The pulse is rapid, the temperature elevated and the skin hot and moist. The calf muscles may be tender to pressure because of peripheral neuropathy. Epileptiform seizures may occur. There is confusion, disorientation and terrifying visual and auditory hallucinations.

Treatment includes the abrupt withdrawal of alcohol; and experience with adrenal steroids has been most gratifying. They control symptoms rapidly and not infrequently have appeared to be life-saving. The dosage should be in the maximal range and may be given orally or parenterally. Clinical results seem to be comparable with the various steroid preparations. Since the treatment is short-term, routine precautions suffice.

The results with chlorpromazine and promazine in the treatment of delirium tremens are equally rewarding. Enough should be used to adequately control the symptoms—usually a matter of individual variation. The need for sedatives and hypnosis has been significantly reduced with the above regimens.

In the management of delirium tremens care must be taken to insure adequate fluid and electrolyte intake, and intravenous administration is usually indicated.

Deficiencies of vitamins are not specific in the causation of delirium tremens, nor will the administration of these vitamins directly relieve it. However, vitamin deficiency is a factor of considerable importance in producing other nutritional disturbances of the nervous system (Wernicke's syndrome, encephalopathy of nicotinic acid deficiency, and peripheral neuropathy). Because of the increased metabolic requirements, clinically latent deficiency states may become manifest. Therefore, thiamine and nicotinic acid as well as the entire vitamin B complex should be given to all patients with delirium tremens to prevent development of the above complications, and perhaps to prevent the development of as yet unknown types of encephalopathy related to nutritional disturbances. Lumbar punctures should be performed for diagnostic purposes only. Other complicating and precipitating factors are treated with specific therapy.

KORSAKOFF'S PSYCHOSIS

According to Wortis and Jolliffe,[10] the role of thiamine in Korsakoff's psychosis is still to be determined. This psychosis consists in deficient power of memory retention for recent events and disorientation in regard to time, place and person, with a tendency to confabulation. When the patient is asked what he did yesterday, and is unable because of his poor memory to recall what he actually did, he invents a story. The logic of the invented story is often ludicrous. The psychosis may or may not be associated with peripheral neuropathy. Although most commonly associated with chronic alcoholism, it is encountered in conjunction with many other conditions (e.g., head injury, arteriosclerosis, subarachnoid bleeding, and toxic and drug psychoses).

Management consists of the following procedures: hospitalization to protect the patient because of psychiatric disability and to prevent further drinking, treatment of peripheral neuropathy and other complications of alcoholism, and high calorie and vitamin diet with supplementary thiamine and total vitamin B complex.

CONVULSIVE DISORDERS

It is generally thought that chronic alcoholism is rarely the cause of epilepsy, although acute alcoholism frequently precipitates convulsions in the epileptic patient. Not infrequently, epileptic patients with organic brain disease who have been relieved of their attacks by surgical and medical therapy suffer a relapse after drinking. Beer and light wines seem to be just as injurious as spirits.

It is widely accepted that convulsions in chronic alcoholic patients are explained by latent epilepsy or an epileptic constitution. According to Taterka, however, chronic alcoholism or alcoholic bouts may cause seizures without any constitutional epileptic pattern. This point of view is supported by the fact that in most of his patients Taterka did not find any characteristic electroencephalographic changes suggesting paroxysmal patterns.[8] Of course, abrupt withdrawal of alcohol is indicated, and seizures should be controlled by anticonvulsants (Dilantin, Mesantoin, barbiturates) as in other convulsive disorders.

ACUTE HALLUCINOSIS [6]

Since excessive indulgence in alcohol can cause acute hallucinosis, it has usually been classified as an alcoholic psychosis. The present tendency is to look upon it as a psychophysiologic reaction liberated by alcoholic excess rather than as a purely toxic manifestation. In some instances it appears that the disorder is a schizophrenic reaction released by alcohol. Acute alcoholic hallucinosis develops only after the prolonged and excessive use of alcohol. The reaction is that of auditory hallucinosis occurring in a clear sensorium and accompanied by marked fear. Hallucinations are usually accusatory, threatening, or both. The voices often refer to the patient in the third person and threaten him with such expressions as "There he is! Let's cut him up!" There may be olfactory or visual hallucinations, and allusions of sight. The patient accepts the hallucinations as reality: ideas of reference, misinterpretations, and the delusional system soon develop. The patient may appeal to the police for protection or arm himself in self-defense. In contrast to delirium tremens, the patient knows accurately his orientation in time, place and person. Further, after recovery there is no amnesia for events occurring during the illness. The patient is usually apprehensive and fearful of his imaginary pursuers, or depressed in reaction to the accusing voices. He may make suicidal attempts to avoid these threats.

Recovery from alcoholic hallucinosis usually occurs in five days to one month. Recurrences are common if the patient again drinks excessively. Not infrequently alcoholic hallucinosis may continue beyond this period and it may merge into a manifest schizophrenia.

Treatment consists in placing the patient under such supervision that he can not harm others or himself. All alcohol must, of course, be withdrawn. Ataractics and sedation are of value, and physical measures such as flow baths may be useful.

ALCOHOLIC DETERIORATION [6]

The drinking of large amounts of alcohol over a long period of time may result in progressive, chronic parenchymatous cerebral degeneration (encephalopathy) with a clinical picture that results from the basic personality defects—with the addition of intellect and memory changes which are consequent upon the organic changes. The loss of control occasioned by alcoholic deterioration may reveal underlying personality deviations. The resultant clinical picture is that of organic change, with loss of memory or confusion in addition to the more usual characteristics found in the alcoholic but manifested to a more severe degree. These may include impulsive behavior, lack of perseverance in endeavor, unreliability, deception, projection of failure onto others, exaggeration of achievements, loss of ambition, carelessness in personal appearance, neglect of family and work responsibilities, irritability, sexual failure, incapacity for sustained attention, etc.

If the above changes are noted early, and if the use of alcohol is discontinued before it has caused irreversible cerebral damage, there may be nearly complete restoration to former health. If severe dementia is present, it may be irreversible.

Hospitalization is usually necessary to prevent further use of alcohol and to prevent dangerous behavior. If, after a long period of hospitalization, a sufficient reversal of changes has occurred to make the patient cooperative, he should be treated by a combined medico-social approach suitable for his own particular needs.

ALCOHOLIC PARANOID STATE [6]

This illness is characterized by jealousy and delusions of infidelity. The patient is irritable, fault-finding, and distrustful. He makes accusations of marital infidelity although there may be little or no evidence to support such accusations. The patient may devise schemes to trap his wife and her supposed lover. This may relate to the patient's own sexual impotence, be a projection of his own desires for extramarital sexual experience, or a combination of both—for not infrequently they coexist.

The prognosis in the alcoholic paranoid states is not good, but removal to the hospital may be followed by improvement. Frequently the patient may dissimulate and maintain that he now recognizes that he was in error and he no longer doubts the fidelity of his wife. After the return to the old situation, however, the former delusions and threatening behavior soon reappear. The fundamental defect is the use of projective mechanisms to blame others for the subject's own inadequacies and prohibited desires. Alcohol facilitates and accentuates the tendency to project.

REFERENCES

1. FELDMAN, D. J., AND ZUCKER, H. D.: Present day medical management of alcoholism. J.A.M.A. *153:* 895, 1953.
2. JELLINEK, E. M.: Effects of Alcohol on the Individual. New Haven, Yale University Press, 1942.
3. JOLLIFFE, N., BOWMAN, K. M., ROSENBLUM, L. A., AND FEIN, H. D.: Nicotinic acid deficiency encephalopathy. J.A.M.A., *114:* 307, 1940.
4. KING, L. S., AND MEEHAN, M. C.: Primary Degeneration of corpus callosum; (Marchiafava's disease). Arch. Neurol. & Psychiat., *36:* 547, 1936.
5. MERRITT, H. H., METLER, F. A., AND PUTNAM, I. J.: Fundamentals of Clinical Neurology. Philadelphia, Blakiston Co., 1947.
6. NOYES, A. P.: Modern Clinical Psychiatry. Philadelphia, W. B. Saunders, 1953.
7. RUSK, H. A.: Rehabilitation Medicine, St. Louis, Mo., C. V. Mosby, 1958.
8. TATERKA, J.: Personal Communication.
9. WERNICKE, K.: Lehrbuch der Gehirnkrankheiten *II*. Kassell, 1881.
10. WORTIS, H., AND JOLLIFFE, N.: New York State J. Med., *41:* 1461, 1941.

IV   *The Psychology of Alcoholism*

In CHAPTER II (An Orientation to Alcoholism as a Disease) it was concluded that psychological factors are of central importance in the etiology of alcoholism. The further discussion of the psychology of alcoholism begins with the following considerations: medical, neuropsychiatric, social and additional psychological complications *following* the prolonged use of excessive amounts of alcohol. What psychological factors underlie the alcoholic's impulse to drink despite these inevitable catastrophic consequences, known to him from his previous experience with alcohol? How can one account for the continuation of drinking for weeks or months as compared to the drinking behavior of the social drinker?

SOME PSYCHIC EFFECTS OF ALCOHOL

To begin with, the special appeal of alcohol for the alcoholic is in part comprehensible on the basis of alcohol's extraordinary psychological effects. Feelings of depression, resentment, anxiety, boredom and unpleasant excitement are all quickly and effectively allayed—at least temporarily—with a few drinks. Alcohol banishes conscience with its self-criticism and concern, thereby removing inhibition and allowing for greater freedom of feeling and action. It has not been sufficiently emphasized, however, that alcohol also has the effect of "dissolving" other mental functions such as the capacity to discriminate between subjective experiences and reality (reality testing). An extreme example of this is in delirium tremens where the alcoholic sees "pink elephants" or snakes. Another example is the short alcoholic who, while intoxicated, neglects the reality of his limited physical strengths, thinks of himself as large and superhumanly powerful, and wants to fight a whole group of men. This last example also illustrates the loss of a realistic *concept of self*. It can also be used to exemplify alcohol's effect of removing *repression*—the mental mechanism whereby desires, impulses and thoughts are pushed down from the field of conscious awareness. Thus, in the example given, the alcoholic becomes aware of aggressive feelings which he now *acts out* by actually getting into a fight. Ordinarily much of one's energy and interests are used for socially useful purposes such as relations with people, work and hobbies. These are called *sublimations*. With alcohol, these sublimations are lost or changed.

29

To summarize what has been said so far: alcohol tends to dissolve conscience and various mental functions such as reality testing, repression, reasonable self-concept and sublimations. However, these changes occur without aggressive and sexual drives being dampened, so that a person who while sober does not dare to perform desired instinctual acts may gain both satisfaction and relief with the help of alcohol. This is not true for all addicting agents. For example, the effect sought after by morphine addicts is the relief obtained primarily in the further repression of instinctual impulses. While on morphine sexual and aggressive drives are diminished. With alcohol, fulfillments are nearer, either through removal of inhibitions and reality considerations followed by acting out, or through withdrawal from reality to pleasurable daydreams. Thus, it may be said that alcohol allays or prevents psychic distress. Through freedom from self-criticism and concern for consequences, impulses are released and satisfaction and its pleasure achieved.

SOME ASPECTS OF THE PSYCHOLOGY OF THE ALCOHOLIC

Having considered the pharmacologic effects of alcohol on the mental life, the question that now presents itself is: What makes certain people seek alcohol and its effects with such intense desire and drive that it becomes the central interest of their lives to the exclusion of all other more usual pursuits?

The pre-morbid makeup of alcoholics is such that they are especially liable to psychic distress of an intense nature, and at the same time tolerance for psychic pain is markedly reduced. Because of these circumstances their main interest centers around a need for relief. The psychic pain may be subjectively experienced as hopeless depression, frightening paranoid rage, extreme boredom, painful loneliness, or combinations of these feelings. Close study of these various types of subjective feelings usually reveal them to be variations or equivalents of depression, often with paranoid coloring. The reaction of depression or its equivalents occur in such individuals in reaction to even minor frustrations of daily life. In this regard the alcoholic is like a "spoiled child." These relatively unimportant events are typically stressed by the alcoholic as the cause of the depression and drinking. It soon becomes evident to the observer, however, that the psychic misery is mainly determined by inner conflicts and an inability to adequately deal with them.

What is the nature of these conflicts? A valuable lead in answering this question may be found in the events that actually happen to the alcoholic when drinking. One type of alcoholic fights with his wife, beats someone in a barroom fight or is beaten, or injures or is injured in an automobile accident. Another openly engages in exhibitionism, "peeping Tom" activities, promiscuous heterosexuality, or various types of homosexual acts. In some cases such direct acting out of feelings does not occur. Instead, these impulses are experienced in the form of withdrawal to a pleasurable state of rich fantasy. In other instances there occurs withdrawal, without action or conscious thought, to a state of pleasant, warm feelings. Whether the outcome of drinking is the putting into action of sexual and aggressive drives, or withdrawal to pleasant fantasy and a pleasurable feeling state, the point is that relief is experienced from psychic distress and pleasure achieved by way of the satisfying of these needs. The assumption can be made that what the alcoholic does while drinking he has the impulse to do while sober but is prohibited from doing so because of conscience and consideration of consequences, and in any event is in conflict and suffers the psychic pains thereof. He obtains relief from conflict by taking advantage of the pharmacologic effect of alcohol of suspending the functions of self-criticism and reality considerations thereby facilitating the discharge of feelings and ideas in the ways described.

In the "morning after" one sees an exaggerated display of the psychic situation that preceded the drinking. In the "hangover" the alcoholic is typically depressed and self-accusing in relation to the expression of those previously forbidden impulses, and concern for realistic consequences is heightened. With the depression, the situation is the same as before the drinking except that now it is more exaggerated. The self-accusations may now also be supported by reprimands of family, employer or friends. So that once again alcohol offers itself for relief. Thus, the alcoholic repeats the cycle—depression is relieved with alcohol followed by increased depression which is again relieved with more alcohol.

There are, in the course of alcoholism, many variations to this typical sequence of drinking in the evening and exeggerated depression in the morning leading to further drinking. These variations will be indicated in the discussion of the course of the disease in the last part of this chapter.

As has been pointed out, the relieving effect of alcohol is especially sought after by persons who experience intolerable psychic distress mainly in the form of depression. An addiction to alcohol develops and a typical course of events ensues on the basis of subtle mental changes and the establishment of a "relationship with the bottle." Is there a particular personality type in which intolerable depression or its equivalent occur and where alcohol is especially sought as a means of relief? When viewed from the point of basic character makeup, one finds a typical grouping of characteristics that may be termed the self-centered, spoiled child character.

As for the self-centeredness of the alcoholic, the following somewhat different but related features are paramount: (1) egocentricity, (2) insufficient involvement with persons in the environment, and (3) a pathologically immature relationship to these people.

The typical characteristics of the pre-morbid features of the alcoholic fall into the above three categories. Egocentricity covers the attitudes in which the main concern is for one's own pleasures and needs. There is involved a high degree of self-love and self-regard. There are feelings of, or longing for, omnipotence. The needs of others are not considered for other people represent only suppliers of needs. Self-esteem is not founded on real achievements or values but on being loved, supported, encouraged and admired—wooing or threats may be used to achieve these. This type of relationship may be observed with employer or wife. Any minor life frustration is reacted to with extreme hurt and depression and with resentment and rage at the person or persons involved and is followed by retreat from them.

Returning to the central point regarding self-centeredness, it should be emphasized that all people have a certain degree of "normal" or "healthy" self-centeredness that is an extension of infancy. There are, however, some people who have excessive degrees of self-centeredness which evidences itself with the personality traits previously described.

Self-centeredness is especially evident in the infantile character. Every human being in infancy passes through a developmental phase when extreme self-centeredness is expected. The hungry infant is concerned with only himself and his hunger. The main goal is for food and the pleasure of the ensuing sleep and these needs are readily satisfied by someone else—the mother. As far as the infant is concerned the world centers around him. The phrase "his majesty the baby" is an apt one. All that matters is that his needs be supplied. Some individuals retain excessive degrees of these characteristics and in later life when confronted with frustrating experiences they demonstrate more openly these infantile characteristics. As to why some people retain these attitudes, there are constitutional factors and various types of environmental influences. There may have been excessive gratification at this stage in infancy by, for example, an overly protective mother such that the child is insufficiently motivated to achievement on its own. Or severe frustration at this phase of development may lead to a persistent yearning for this stage and its satisfactions. Another possibility is that of excessive satisfactions alternating with undue and excessive frustrations. The wish to be fed is demonstrated on the surface in the alcoholic by the drinking itself and during abstinence by the substitution of extraordinary amounts of food, coffee, soda and candy, leading to increased weight.

As for the wish to sleep, a large percentage of alcoholics have insomnia and a particularly intense preoccupation with it. Many begin their alcoholic careers using alcohol specifically as a somnifacient. In the course of alcoholism, coma as a kind of sleep may be the desired goal, or even while awake and drinking the alcoholic is in a "dreamy state." The high incidence of suicides among alcoholics would appear to be related to the wish for death—imagined as an endless peaceful sleep.

It is striking to observe the alcoholic systematically going about destroying his chances in life. Giving up everything that is ordinarily considered as valuable: physical and mental health, family, friends and occupation. He seems determined to destroy himself and sometimes literally does: in accidents, physical illness or suicide. This points up the commonly observed self-destructive tendencies of the alcoholic. If the goal is return to the fantasy of the helpless infant who will be fed and cared for, any adult abilities, interests and activities only interfere in the achievement of this fantasy state and the unconscious goal is to be rid of them. The use of alcohol is quite unique for this purpose in its impairment of all mature functions, stimulation of fantasy, and actual achievement of helplessness with its attendant attention and concern on the part of all those close to the alcoholic. An actualization of the mother-child arrangement can be seen, for example, when the alcoholic is in the hospital bed, being fed and cared for by a kind nurse.

Although it may be said that the infantile character lies behind alcoholism, it is also true that in many other clinical entities one finds this constellation. This then leads to the question of why the choice of alcoholism rather than open depression, elation, schizophrenia, or perversion. Although a complete answer cannot be given, the following factors appear to be important: There is the choice of alcoholism as an aspect of emulating an alcoholic parent. In addition, there may be highly specific psychological differences in the infantile character that results in the turning to alcoholism rather than to some other neurosis.

SPECIAL PERSONALITY FEATURES OF THE ALCOHOLIC PATIENT IN INDUSTRY

Previous discussion concerned itself with the psychology of the alcoholic in general. What follows is a discussion of the special features of the psychology of the alcoholic seen in industry. These data are derived from the clinical examinations and psychological testing of approximately one hundred and fifty alcoholics referred by various industries to the Consultation Clinic for Alcoholism. (See CHAPTER VII).

The alcoholic patients seen at the Consultation Clinic present a variety of personality pictures from neurotic to psychotic and encompass almost all of the nosological groups. These patients are as divergent as any unselected group of people might be, yet certain characteristics or traits persist throughout the many diagnostic categories. It should be emphasized that we are describing one group of alcoholic patients from industry with special features. Material concerning personality factors has been collected in clinical interviews and corroborated by psychological tests. Compiling this material from projective psychological tests enables us to describe a typical or average group of alcoholic patients in industry. Also, as in every attempt to generalize on personality and human behavior, there are many exceptions to the description presented below.

This is a notably unproductive, unimaginative, and constricted group of people lacking in insight and presenting in general a picture of widespread restriction of interests and activity. Their anxiety is deeply embedded—constituting an underlying source of motivation affecting their functioning in almost every area of living. They strenuously resist self-examination, delimit inner ideation, and restrict generally their awareness of all the aspects of living. They initiate little on their own, and their activities are sustained largely by dint of external pressures. They expound strictly conventional points of view and are primarily guided in their behavior by what they think is expected of them. They reveal an inadequately developed sense of self and show a corresponding incapacity for empathizing with other people. Their understanding of their own motivational system is shallow because so much is withheld from consciousness. They dread their impulses and cannot even tolerate their own ideas. Privately entertained deliberations arouse as much anxiety and guilt as overt behavior. Their adjustment is based on the rigid formula "hear no evil, speak no evil, see no evil."

Few of these patients are appreciative of the fact that they are capable of self-direction; few wonder about their role in life or give any thought to their relationships with others. They move about in their interpersonal environment as if they were in a haze, never permitting relationships to crystallize. Eventually their understanding of social cause and effect weakens and they regard external events as having happened fortuitously —almost magically. By and large, their attention is confined to what is mundane and obvious. Living becomes a tedious, humdrum affair that must be periodically interrupted by some form of release or a burst of activity. Their inhibition and virtual annihilation of fantasy activity and inner thought is often an expression of denial. To avoid contemplation of a problem is to reduce its impact, to remove it from the self. The conviction that problems do not originate with the self is further reinforced by the externalization of difficulties.

They are immature people who cannot withstand the frustration of instinctual impulses. They are equally intolerant of delayed gratification and are impulsively self-indulgent. Thus, they have to contend with strong pressure of conscience and are endlessly caught up in guilt feelings. These guilt feelings do not effectively regulate or restrain them in their activities, but serve as a backdrop against which they operate. Guilt feelings precede gratification in the anticipation of punishment and follow in the wake of indulgence. Their pleasurable activities are thus circumscribed by a concern with punishment. Only a partial and incomplete satisfaction can be experienced in such an emotional context. Continued preoccupation with instinctual needs results in the deflection of energies from the pursuit of more mature social goals.

They are intolerant of compromise solutions and are possessed of a moral sense that is sharply dichotomous, providing only for blacks and whites. They are fitfully perfectionistic, disparaging of their activities and irritated by ambiguity and uncertainty. Within circumscribed areas of living, they are inclined to be effectively compulsive and are capable of carefully planned, methodical, routinized behavior which undoubtedly contributes to their job efficiency.

They desire to achieve but they cannot independently evolve a manner of operation or persist in the fact of difficulty. They may establish lofty goals but usually fail to work out the means of achieving them. Similarly, they evidence a limited capacity for projecting themselves into the future so as to anticipate arising eventualities and consequences. They typically rush into situations in a head-on fashion, stopping only to formulate global and superficial impressions. They must, as it were, take it all in at the initial encounter. The complex and the simple situation meet essentially with the same incorporative approach. This consideration of a totality, this need to engage in vague planning activities, gives them the feeling that they are controlling the situation, that they are manipulating things to their own advantage and yields a spurious sense of omnipotence. Such an approach, however, forestalls serious and prolonged involvement with problems and bespeaks a fly-by-night kind of interaction with the environment.

THE COURSE OF ALCOHOLISM *

The course of the disease, alcoholism, is considered in the light of the preceding discussion of the psychology of the alcoholic. The phases and sequence of the phenomena were worked out by Jellinek, on the basis of a questionnaire study of two thousand alcoholics. He points out that the phenomena and sequence are only indications of an average trend. In the discussion that follows this writer elaborates on the interpretations of the phenomena—in italics.

The pre-alcoholic phase

Partly through denial and in part due to increased sociability caused by alcohol, the alcoholic at first tends to ascribe relief to the social situation in which drinking occurs. Later he becomes consciously aware of the direct connection between drinking and the relief. In the beginning, relief in drinking is sought occasionally only, but in the course of six months to two years drinking affects regressive changes which, although still minimal, bring about greater conflict and depression and greater reliance on alcohol resulting in daily drinking. This involves heavy drinking, but gross overt intoxication does not result; by evening the drinker feels comfortable. Drinking is as yet not conspicuous to associates nor does it seem like a serious problem to the drinker. However, an increase in alcohol tolerance is noted that requires larger amounts of alcohol than formerly to achieve the desired effects. The above stage of occasional and constant drinking lasts from several months to two years.

* Numbers in parentheses refer to the sequence of phenomena as described by Jellinek.

The prodromal phase

There now occurs episodes of *alcoholic amnesia* (1) *"blackouts".* The alcoholic may, while drinking, carry on a reasonable conversation or engage in complicated activities without appearing intoxicated and then have a complete loss of memory about either the following morning. The amnesia may become evident to the alcoholic only when a comment is made by someone regarding the previous evening, or the patient may wake up and be spontaneously aware of an inability to remember where he had been or how he got home. The usual reaction to the realization of amnesia is fright. The amnesia for the evening may remain indefinitely or may be pieced together from a few spotty recollections and information given by others. Alcoholic amnesia may occur occasionally in social drinkers, especially with large amounts of alcohol. It is the frequency of "blackouts" with even moderate amounts of alcohol that marks the alcoholic. While toxic factors contribute to alcoholic amnesia, there is no doubt that psychological factors are important. From a psychological point of view "blackouts" represent the pushing-out of awareness forbidden thoughts and effects. The state of intoxication also facilitates amnesia by impairing memory.

At about this same time drinking behavior is such as to indicate a strong need for and conflict about alcohol. There are *surreptitious drinking* (2) ; *preoccupation with alcohol* (3) ; *avid drinking* (gulping of the first few drinks) (4) ; *guilt feeling about mode of drinking* (5) ; *the avoidance of reference to alcohol in conversation* (6). These features, together with an *increasing frequency of alcoholic amnesia* (7), foreshadow the development of a marked addiction. They are premonitory signs and this period may be called the prodromal phase of alcohol addiction. In this phase alcohol consumption is large and continuous, leading to a state of emotional anesthesia by evening. However, there is not gross and overt indication of intoxication. Guilt feelings and defensiveness regarding drinking, and the giving-up of personal relations, are the first signs of the serious involvement with alcohol. At this point rationalizations of drinking are neither strong nor highly organized. There is still some insight as well as fear of possible consequences. The prodromal period may last anywhere from six months to four or five years. The prodromal phase ends and the crucial phase begins with the onset of loss of control of drinking—the critical sign of alcohol addiction.

The crucial phase

With *loss of control* (8) any drinking starts a chain reaction of further drinking based on an intense craving. The bout of drinking continues until the drinker is too intoxicated or sick to ingest more alcohol. A drinking bout may not be started by any conscious psychological need of the moment but rather by a "social" drink. In other instances, the impulse to drink outside of a social situation results in the first drink, following which loss of control occurs. The idea of loss of control is not acceptable to the alcoholic and this becomes an additional source of psychic distress and adds to the desire for the first drink, with the hope and conviction via denial that loss of control will not occur. The desire is to master the loss of control and to be a social drinker. With the onset of loss of control the alcohol addict begins to *rationalize his drinking behavior* (9), producing the well known alcoholic "alibis". He finds explanations to convince himself that he had good reason to get intoxicated and that it was not a matter of unmanageable craving following the first drink. An entire system of rationalizations is elaborated both for the alcoholic and to counteract *social pressures* (10) which now begin. The drinking behavior has now become conspicuous and wife, employer and friends begin to reprove and warn the drinker. At this point, despite rationalizations, loss of self-esteem along with overt indications of self-centeredness occurs and leads to *grandiose behavior* (11) and attitudes, for example, spending large amounts of money and pretending to be wealthy. Along with rationalization and denial there occurs projection —ascribing all difficulties to others. This paranoid picture is marked by *aggressive behavior* (12). For example, getting into numerous fights. This contributes to further guilt feelings and now *persistent remorse* (13) arises, leading to further drinking. Because of fear of disintegration and social pressures, the addict now goes on *periods of total abstinence* (14) or "experiments" with *changing the pattern of his drinking* (15) by setting rules about not drinking before a certain hour of the day, with only his wife, drinking only beer or wine and so forth. With increasing hostility he *drops friends* (16) and *quits jobs,* (17) in part because of anticipating on the basis of projection that he will be abandoned by those who he erroneously believes dislike him.

Withdrawal and personal isolation become more pronounced as his entire *behavior becomes alcohol-centered* (18). Interest centers about how activities might interfere with drinking rather than how drinking might interfere with activities. With increasing self-centeredness and preoccupation with alcohol there ensues *loss of outside interests* (19) and a *reinterpretation of personal relations* (20). For example, the alcoholic may think over his relation with a close friend and now decide that his friend has really been his enemy for many years. As part of the feeling of being "let down" by friends and family, there ensues marked *self-pity* (21) and there may be contemplated or actual *geographic escape* (22). *A change in family habits* (23) then occurs: The wife and children may withdraw from social life for fear of embarrassment or contrariwise may escape from the difficult home situation into intense social activities. These actions now contribute to realistic bases for further *unreasonable resentments* (24) in the alcoholic.

The central concern with alcohol induces the addict to *protect his supply* (25), i.e., to lay in large stocks of alcohol and to hide bottles in unthought-of places. *Neglect of proper nutrition* (26), together with the toxic effects of heavy drinking, now contribute to the development of medical complaints and the *first hospitalization* (27).

A usual effect is a *decrease of the sexual drive* (28) giving rise to *alcoholic jealousy* (29) towards the wife, with unwarranted accusations of infidelity. By this time the alcoholic is so burdened with conflict and distress that he is unable to start the day without first having a drink. Regular *morning drinking* (30) marks the end of the crucial phase and the beginning of the chronic phase.

The chronic phase

Prolonged intoxications (31) now occur, leading to *marked ethical deterioration* (32) and gross *impairment of thinking* (33). At this time *alcoholic psychosis* (34) occurs in approximately ten per cent of all alcoholics. The alcoholic now seeks out and *drinks with persons far below his social level* (35) and if nothing else is available drinks *"technical products"* (36) such as bay rum or rubbing alcohol. A *loss of tolerance* (37) occurs so that even smaller amounts of alcohol may be sufficient to bring about a stuporous state. Without alcohol *indefinable fears* (38) and *tremors* (39) become persistent and the alcoholic is focussed on controlling these with alcohol. This also applies to *psychomotor inhibition* (40), the inability to initiate a simple mechanical act, such as winding a watch, in the absence of alcohol. Now more gross, *drinking takes on an obsessive character* (41).

In sixty per cent of alcoholics some *vague religious desires develop* (42) in an effort to maintain intactness. These may take the form of religious ideas or an attempt to return to one's church, but the *entire rationalization system fails* (43) finally, along with the collapse of other psychological defenses. The addict now feels defeated and is spontaneously accessible to treatment.

REFERENCES

BERNSTEIN, I.: The role of narcissim in moral masochism. Psychoanal. Quart. *26:* 3, 1957.

FENICHEL, O.: The Psychoanalytic Theory of the Neurosis. New York, W. W. Norton & Co., 1946.

JELLINEK, E. M.: Phases of alcohol addiction. Quart. J. Stud. Alcohol *13:* 673–684, 1952.

LEWIN, B. D.: The Psychoanalysis of Elation. New York, W. W. Norton & Co., 1950.

LOEWENSTEIN, R.: Psychoanalytic theory of masochism. J. Am. Psychoanal. Assoc. *5:* (2), April, 1957.

RADO, S.: The psychoanalysis of pharmacothymia (drug addiction). Psychoanal. Quart. *2:* (1), January, 1933.

V *Psychological Treatment for Alcoholism*

MOTIVATION FOR TREATMENT [6, 11]

THE EXTENT of motivation for treatment, especially for total and permanent abstinence, is of crucial importance in the outcome of the treatment of the alcoholic patient.

One typical attitude of the alcoholic is denial of alcoholism or that drinking has created physical and mental problems for him at work and at home. Since he does not regard his drinking as a serious problem he refuses treatment or else comes to treatment, in whatever form it may take, in a reluctant and uncooperative mood—perhaps only to satisfy his wife or some other person. The lack of proper and sufficient motivation for treatment is clearly connected with the use of the mechanism of denial; * he has no deep or consistent conviction that he is an alcoholic and needs assistance. Since he is not convinced, he has little motivation to seek help.

Many alcoholics manage to maintain their denial and fail to recognize their problems, doing nothing constructive about them until they have lost everything. Efforts of various sorts in their behalf may have been made without avail. Such patients seem to have to reach "low-bottom" before the realities of their situation dawn on them. When this occurs the situation may be more hopeful in the sense that they now genuinely seek help. In many such instances all the physician or family can do is to stand by and hope that the downward spiralling process will be quick and not too disastrous, and will result in an earnest desire to be well.

In recent years interest has centered on the possibilities of undoing denial and establishing positive motivation in the alcoholic before the whole gamut of the illness has been run and before the phase of "low-bottom" has been reached.

It is striking to see how, just since 1952, industry can be effective in assisting in undoing denials and establishing positive motivation in

_____

* By "denial" is meant the mental mechanism whereby unpleasant realities are not fully unconsciously perceived, as opposed to malingering or lying.

41

alcoholics. The result in most cases is real improvement for the alcoholic and an advantage for industry in keeping a valuable employee. After several warnings, the employee is placed on probation with the understanding that should further difficulties arise involving drinking he will be fired. At the same time he is offered treatment at the Consultation Clinic for Alcoholism (New York University-Bellevue Medical Center). For the employee who has worked for a particular company for an average of twenty-three years, with the advantages thereof, the effect is usually immediate. For the most part these patients respond rapidly to this approach. They face up squarely to the consequences of their drinking, become well motivated and are then treatable before job and everything else has been lost. The principle involved is that of realistically restricting or applying pressure in individually meaningful areas and at the same time offering proper help. It is understood, of course, that the restrictions or pressures applied are warranted by the actual behavior of the alcoholic. For example, in industry there is not only work inefficiency, absenteeism, and damaging of materials, but, in some instances—the endangering of lives. The physician who sees the alcoholic in practice is able in some instances to apply the same procedure. By discussion with a well-meaning employer, the reality of the employer's intention to fire can be conveyed to the patient at the same time that medical assistance is offered.

The same principle has been used in courts where alcoholics may be placed on probation rather than jailed, provided they seek help. Naturally this is effective only in those who have strong feelings against going to jail. The use of job and court probation is the more direct application of the principle indicated in the clinical experience cited.

What are some other ways in which the physician can make use of this principle? When examination of the alcoholic reveals the complications of alcoholism, e.g., cirrhosis, gastritis or peripheral neuropathy, the patient should be informed; and the serious implications of these medical complications should be fully explained. Many an alcoholic has taken such information seriously, although initially most do not. Alcoholics who are impressed and seriously motivated by this information are those who tend to be more concerned about body health. The first episode of delirium tremens or the first hospitalization for a psychiatric complication of alcoholism will, in some, elicit cognizance of the illness and positive motivation. In some alcoholics, separation from spouse is advisable as a safeguard for spouse and children. It may also result, in those alcoholics for whom the family is meaningful, in a surging up of positive motivation.

Realistic and increased concern may follow the first "blackout"— alcoholic amnesia. Typically, the alcoholic is frightened at the things he may have done the previous night but cannot remember. A serious accident while drinking may elicit increased motivation. The "hangover" is a phase in which the alcoholic is more apt to be amenable to starting a treatment program. The physician can assist in the undoing of denial and development of motivation; and he should be available if and when the alcoholic becomes motivated for one or another reason. While it is best if the alcoholic is well motivated when first seen by the physician, this is not entirely necessary. It may be the first step to develop such motivation. Much depends on the physician's attitudes: being harsh and critical will elicit more denial; an objective and sympathetic attitude will lessen denial. The physician should not be the one to restrict the patient. In industry, restrictions and prohibitions should come from management, leaving the physician free to gain the patient's cooperation so that adequate medical care can be administered.

THE PSYCHOTHERAPIES

In a small volume covering many aspects of alcoholism, it would not be feasible to elaborate in detail on the technical aspects of the various types of psychotherapy for the alcoholic. One may only discuss some of the general principles and useful types of treatment.

Although each alcoholic has his own particular symptoms, character defects, potentialities, limitations and reality problems, there is value in the psychotherapist's being aware of the typical features of alcoholics in general. These have been discussed in the previous section on the psychology of the alcoholic and are here summarized. The alcoholic is typically found to be essentially an infantile, self-centered individual. The image of himself is one of either omnipotence or of being small and incompetent. He is impatient of delay, intolerant of frustration and impulsive. He is sensitive and easily offended. Personal relations are tenuous and difficult; the alcoholic tends to be self-destructive and may be openly or insidiously provocative. There is in treatment the ever-present possibility too, of drinking and becoming worse, and interruption of treatment is common. Depressive and paranoid trends are usually evident; and one must be aware of the possibility of psychotic features.

The determination of which particular type of psychotherapy is best suited for the needs of a particular patient can be determined only on the basis of a careful evaluation of the above features as well as the life situation, age, intelligence and motivation. Depending on such an over-all evaluation, and if all factors are favorable, the psychiatrist may decide upon thoroughgoing revision of character difficulties. Or indications may point to the desirability of analysis of particular aspects in a circum-scribed fashion. Other possibilities include directive-supportive psycho-therapy (where guidance and advice are emphasized), group psy-chotherapy, or psychotherapy that has as its goal joining Alcoholics Anonymous. A constant and continuing problem for the alcoholic in psy-chotherapy is the losing sight of reality problems, denial of alcoholism and loss of positive motivation. While this is true in a sense for all psy-chiatric patients, it is especially pertinent for the alcoholic on the basis of his particular makeup.

Some, but not all, physicians and psychiatrists with varying theoreti-cal points of view are able to effect improvements or "cures" in alco-holics. A central requirement is that the therapist be genuinely interested in treating the alcoholic and be willing to accept the inevitable frustra-tions of drinking bouts while the patient is in treatment, phone calls at night, etc. It is important that the therapist feel neither threatened and hostile nor overly sympathetic to the alcoholic especially in relation to expected acting out. The physician or psychiatrist who experiences un-manageable hostility toward the alcoholic should transfer the patient to someone else.

Psychotherapy and Antabuse are often used concurrently. It is often useful and possible for the patient to be both in psychotherapy and Alcoholics Anonymous. Generally speaking, these methods of treatment are not mutually exclusive.

PSYCHOANALYSIS

Except for the particularly suitable patient (intelligent and not severely disturbed) analysis is not applicable for most true alcoholics. On the other hand, many a patient for whom drinking is mainly a symptom of another neurosis is quite manageable with this form of treatment. The difficulties in analysis of the patient who is essentially an alcoholic stem from his intolerance for frustration, tendency to go into action—breaking off of treatment, going on a drinking bout, or usually both. In the course of treatment the patient often loses sight of the therapeutic nature of the treatment situation and reacts to fantasies and feelings about the analyst as if they were realities. Knight has reported on a series of alcoholics analyzed within a hospital. In some instances this approach is indicated; in others only a preliminary period of analysis in a hospital is preferable. In some instances it is best that the patient first be abstinent before analysis begins; in others it may be wiser to insist on abstinence soon after treatment begins. In still others it is best not to interfere in this way but to simply analyze. At a later phase of the analysis, the patient may be better prepared to give up his involvement with alcohol. Which of these procedures is selected can be determined only on the basis of a careful consideration of the multiplicity of factors involved. In general, the analysis of the alcoholic requires sufficient flexibility to make modifications in treatment in accordance with carefully considered needs of the individual patient.

It should be noted that although psychoanalysis has certain limitations in its applicability in the *therapy* of alcoholics, this in no way detracts from the validity and usefulness of its theory as applied to modified forms of psychoanalysis and other therapeutic approaches for the alcoholic. A close examination of valuable procedures such as Alcoholics Anonymous, group psychotherapy, and some medical procedures, demonstrate the application of concepts that coincide with basic analytic thinking.

GROUP PSYCHOTHERAPY [6, 8, 9, 10]

In recent years, widespread interest has developed in the use of group psychotherapy for alcoholics. For many alcoholics the intensity of feelings toward the analyst in the analytic situation is beyond their tolerance. In group psychotherapy these feelings are diluted. The patient develops feelings and attitudes towards other patients as well as towards the therapist—both the former and latter being analyzable. Underneath his shell, the alcoholic is typically a severely guilt-ridden person and considers himself often as totally different and bad compared to other alcoholics and, certainly, to non-alcoholics. It is relieving for him to hear described, in the group, the inner feelings and experiences of other alcoholics; to understand that he is not the only person in the world to have had such difficulties. Reasonable personal relations are developed among patients and with the therapist, and these reflect upon attitudes outside of treatment. A patient who initially feels timorous about the expression of an aggressive feeling may first try it out on another patient, or supported by other patients with similar feelings may then be able to express it directly to the therapist, which can then lead to its analysis. It may be said that in group therapy of an analytic type, feelings develop which are within the confines of the alcoholic's low tolerance and at the same time are sufficiently intense for therapeutic purposes. In some instances, patients have continued with proper individual analysis following a period of group psychotherapy.

Several different types of group psychotherapy have been reported: didactic-discussion (McCarthy); didactic-discussion with the goal of having the patient accept Alcoholics Anonymous (Heath); repressional-inspirational (Mueller); and analytic group psychotherapy (Pfeffer, Friedland, Wortis). Alcoholics Anonymous may be considered an inspirational-supportive type of group psychotherapy. While adequately controlled studies are not yet available, it appears that all of these approaches help at least some alcoholics. The two types of group psychotherapy most generally used are directive-supportive and analytic.

In DIRECTIVE-SUPPORTIVE GROUP PSYCHOTHERAPY the group usually numbers about twelve patients, and the therapeutic work is kept more on a discussion level because it is felt that these particular patients for various reasons should not have deeper probing. The considerations for this choice of treatment are essentially those discussed under individual directive-supportive therapy.

In ANALYTIC GROUP PSYCHOTHERAPY the group usually consists of about eight patients who are considered essentially neurotic drinkers who can be helped more effectively by intensive work. These patients are seen in a group twice a week, each session of approximately one hour's duration. There are some general advantages in treating the alcoholic in a group because so often he is a hostile, anxious, guilt-ridden person with feelings that he alone experiences disturbing emotions and ideas. The patient is encouraged and stimulated by the presence of other people willing to express, explore and evaluate all sorts of previously hidden feelings. In the group, he has the opportunity of observing similar problems in others, permitting increased insight into his own problems and gradual establishment of relationships with others. These relationships develop not only with the therapist but with other patients, and the motivations and nature of these relationships are also analyzed. As relationships are formed in less distorted fashion in the group, the patient is frequently able to establish similarly positive emotional ties at home and at work.

INDIVIDUAL PSYCHOTHERAPY [1, 2, 4]

Psychoanalysis has already been considered. In addition, there are directive-supportive and analytic psychotherapy. The indications for one or a combination of these should depend entirely on the needs of the patient.

INDIVIDUAL DIRECTIVE-SUPPORTIVE PSYCHOTHERAPY is carried on with patients who mainly require discussion about their drinking problem and understanding of how their drinking has led to their many difficulties, including the possibility of job loss, family problems, debt and poor health. The inability of an alcoholic to use alcohol in any form is emphasized. The patient is encouraged to defend himself against the desire for the first drink, to associate with non-drinking friends, and an attempt is made to interest him in useful hobbies. Undoubtedly, one of the centrally important features of this particular approach is the rapport established between physician and patient, with the patient regarding the physician as a friend and a wise counsellor. The patient usually is very grateful for this and in large part makes an effort to help himself as a way of pleasing and showing appreciation to the physician. Of the various rational or reasonable appeals to the patient to solve his drinking problem, the one that has proven most useful is the emphasis on the advantages of keeping his present job. This type of treatment is appropriate for those patients where neurotic difficulties are such that more intensive probing is unnecessary or contraindicated. It is indicated in cases where the intellectual level is quite low or where potential psychosis precludes deeper probing. In this form of treatment, patients are usually seen one to three times a week.

In INDIVIDUAL ANALYTIC PSYCHOTHERAPY many of the same techniques are used as in individual psychotherapy with the addition of deeper probing and analysis. The patient is made conscious of conflicts and motivations of which he was formerly unaware, providing for a decrease in tension and consequent diminution of the need to drink. One patient, whose main complaint was of being extremely anxious whenever his wife went out of the house, and who had fears that something terrible would happen to her, was considered more suitable for individual analytic psychotherapy; other indications were also present. The patient was encouraged to talk freely, and gradually it was possible to demonstrate in a meaningful way to the patient that his fears concerning his wife were related to repressed feelings of anger toward her and his previously unknown wish that something should happen to her. Bringing these feelings to light permitted the patient to deal with them in a more constructive manner and to alleviate his fear.

ALCOHOLICS ANONYMOUS [5]

This important organization was begun in 1935 by two alcoholics following the principle of self-help. Today Alcoholics Anonymous has over 100,000 members in 1500 groups throughout the United States, Canada and a dozen other countries.

Most physicians who have worked intimately with alcoholics are favorably impressed with the intent, approach and results of Alcoholics Anonymous. Members of A.A. are a readily available resource for assistance with an alcoholic, and their devotion to the problems of alcoholism is impressive. In some instances, the physician may accomplish an important step if he is able to induce the patient to join A.A. Some industries have made Alcoholics Anonymous the core of their company program (see CHAPTER VII).

The guiding principles for members of A.A. are contained in "The Twelve Steps." Close study of these twelve steps, derived by alcoholics from their own experiences, are in remarkable parallel with some of the principles that the psychiatrist sees as of central importance for the alcoholic.

THE TWELVE STEPS

1. We admitted we were powerless over alcohol—that our lives had become unmanageable.

2. Came to believe that a Power greater than ourselves could restore us to sanity.

3. Made a decision to turn our will and our lives over to the care of God as we understood Him.

4. Made a searching and fearless moral inventory of ourselves.

5. Admitted to God, to ourselves, and to another human being the exact nature of our wrongs.

6. Were entirely ready to have God remove all these defects of character.

7. Humbly asked Him to remove our shortcomings.

8. Made a list of all persons we had harmed, and became willing to make amends to them all.

9. Made direct amends to such people wherever possible, except when to do so would injure them or others.

10. Continued to take personal inventory and when we were wrong promptly admitted it.

11. Sought through prayer and meditation to improve our conscious contact with God as we understood Him, praying only for knowledge of His will for us and the power to carry that out.

12. Having had a spiritual experience as the result of these steps, we tried to carry this message to alcoholics, and to practice these principles in all our affairs.

In considering the first step, for example, one finds contained in it the idea of the undoing of *denial*, that characteristic mental mechanism of the alcoholic which persists in the belief that drinking is controllable despite evidence to the contrary. The alcoholic manages not to be aware of the devastating effects of his drinking in all significant areas of adaptation.

Throughout these twelve steps one sees the factor of *omnipotence* and the goal of giving it up. Steps four and ten, with their suggestion of personal inventory, supply what is so often lacking in the alcoholic—a sufficiently realistic self-evaluation. In steps nine and twelve the important aspect of personal relations are referred to.

In addition to the principles already outlined and discussed, there is for the alcoholic in A.A. the opportunity to implement these by associations with other alcoholics in both the larger "open" meetings and the small "closed" discussion meetings. As indicated previously, the alcoholic tends to feel isolated from people in general—with the feeling that he is completely different, disliked and unaccepted. Thus, it is important as an initial step at least that he have the opportunity to air his problems with other alcoholics; to see that he is not the only one with his special make-up, and his own prohibited and sometimes acted out impulses and fantasies. In addition, he has the opportunity of establishing close and good relationships with the other members of the group. From the human contact experienced in the A.A. group, the alcoholic is equipped to establish more satisfactory relations with family and others.

REFERENCES

1. Fox, R., AND Lyon, P.: Alcoholism. New York, Random House, 1955, pp. 172–180.
2. Kant, F.: The Treatment of the Alcoholic. Springfield, Ill., C. C. Thomas, 1954, pp. 67–76.

3. KNIGHT, R.: The psychoanalytic treatment in a sanatorium of chronic addiction to alcohol. J.A.M.A. *3:* 1938.

4. LOVELL, H.: Hope and Help for the Alcoholic. New York, Doubleday & Co., 1953, pp. 160–167.

5. MANN, M.: Primer on Alcoholism. New York, Rhinehart, 1950.

6. McCARTHY, R.: Group therapy for the treatment of alcoholism. Quart. J. Stud. on Alcohol. *10:* 63, 1949.

7. PFEFFER, A. Z.: Alcoholism and motivation for treatment. Bull. N. J. Acad. Med. *1:* 2–6, 1956.

8. ——, FRIEDLAND, P., AND WORTIS, S. B.: Group psychotherapy for alcoholics. Quart. J. Stud. on Alcohol. *10:* 198, 1949.

9. SCHEIDLINGER, S.: The concept of identification in group psychotherapy. Am. J. Psychotherapy. *9:* 661, 1955.

10. SLAVSON, S. R. et al.: Bibliography on group psychotherapy. Am. Group Therapy Assoc. Vol. I, 1950. (Also see Vol. II, 1954.)

11. TIEBOUT, H.: The act of surrender in the therapeutic process. Quart. J. Stud. on Alcohol. *10:* 48, 1949.

VI   *Adjunctive Treatments and Procedures for Alcoholism*

HOSPITALIZATION

Whether or not an alcoholic patient should be hospitalized depends on various circumstances. His medical condition, the degree of behavior that is destructive to himself and others, the possibilities for treatment outside of a hospital in respect to the availability of medical assistance, and the home situation must be considered. A decision for hospitalization also depends on the over-all planning of the management in a particular case and the degree of cooperation of the patient.

Usually hospitalization is indicated in the disturbed states such as alcoholic deterioration, hallucinosis, delirium tremens, alcoholic coma and some cases of acute intoxication. Hospitalization too early in the course of a drinking bout will sometimes lead to an unmanageable lack of cooperation, whereas later on hospitalization may be accepted readily. Treatment at home is often difficult even when the home is turned into a "hospital" with nurses and careful medical supervision. The alcoholic is often able to get his own way with nurses and family and may manage to obtain alcohol. In some instances treatment at home may be tried with the agreement that should it fail, hospitalization will then be accepted.

Hospitalization offers certain advantages, again depending on the general plan of management. In addition to the ready availability of laboratories and consultants and better control of the patient, the alcoholic, after sobering up, finds himself away from disturbing work and family complications. If good rapport has been established with his physician, the patient can be helped to view more objectively the difficulties that alcoholism has created for him. Hospitalization is sometimes helpful for the family of the alcoholic, enabling them to get their bearings and thereby manage the situation better. Consultation with the relatives of the alcoholic in relation to family and medical planning is usually necessary.

During the period of hospitalization, the alcoholic is most apt to see more realistically the true state of his affairs. Typically, after the distress of the hangover and withdrawal period, the alcoholic again begins to deny his problem with drinking and his own involvement in it. He again tends to insist that he is not an alcoholic, that he won't drink again and that his problems are caused by others. While the patient is hospitalized, advantage should be taken of the opportunity to establish a working relationship with the person who will continue to treat him. Plans may be made for the post-hospital period, many of the usual home, personal or business problems may be clarified and if indicated the patient may be started on Antabuse or other medication.

The type of hospital indicated, will depend on the state of the alcoholic. Cases involving severe alcoholic deterioration are usually best treated in a psychiatric hospital. It should be noted, however, that alcoholics who initially give a clear-cut picture of alcoholic deterioration sometimes clear up sufficiently in several weeks to make discharge from the hospital and outside treatment possible, depending on the clinical picture and the circumstances at home. Psychiatric hospitalization is indicated in cases of continuing psychoses such as Korsakoff's psychosis or chronic hallucinosis. Alcoholics with acute intoxication are treatable in the general hospital with or without special wards, though consideration of how disturbing the alcoholic will be to other patients and the likelihood of his going into one of the acute disturbed alcoholic states must be made. The newer medications, such as the tranquilizers, have enabled more alcoholics to be treated in the general hospital. Some hospitals have arranged for special wards for alcoholics; in other hospitals selected alcoholics are admitted to general wards on the basis of confidence that the referring physician's clinical judgment can be relied on as to the unlikelihood of disturbing behavior, suicide attempts, etc. One useful approach is to have nurses on the case for the first few days, so that there is an opportunity for the patient to get over the initial distress of withdrawal from alcohol, become stabilized on sedatives and/or tranquilizers, get used to the hospital surroundings and establish a firm reliance and relationship to the attending physician. The physician must critically evaluate the optimal length of hospitalization. Hospitalization can be overdone. For example, hospitalization of an alcoholic with uncomplicated acute intoxication for too long may result in increased resentments and desire for revenge with the determination to drink on discharge.

ANTABUSE [1]

Antabuse—trade name of tetra-ethyl-thiuram disulphide—known also by other trade names (Disulphiuram, Aversan, Absetinyl, and Refusal) has now been in use in the treatment of chronic alcoholics for eight years. Prior to that it had been used for years as an anti-oxident in the rubber industry. Its effectiveness as an alcohol sensitizing drug was discovered quite accidentally when in the search for an anti-helminthic two Danish workers, Drs. Jacobsen and Hald, dosed themselves with Antabuse. Soon after, they attended a party and after imbibing a cocktail, startled the company by developing tachycardia, dyspnea, palpitations, a lobster-like complexion and red bulging eyes—signs and symptoms aptly referred to in the French literature as "La Maladie Rouge" and now recognized as the alcohol-Antabuse reaction. From a pharmaco-dynamic point of view, TETD (tetra-ethyl-thiuram disul-phide) appears to effect its results by interfering in the metabolism of alcohol at the acetaldehyde stage, resulting in a marked rise in blood acetaldehyde levels. Normally alcohol is oxidized to CO_2 and water. While TETD by itself exerts no change in the blood acetaldehyde levels, when alcohol is ingested following the ingestion of TETD there is a five to tenfold increase in blood acetaldehyde levels. This increase appears due to a decrease in the breakdown of acetaldehyde. Ordinarily, blood acetaledhyde is barely detectable (less than .05 mg. per cent) but after alcohol ingestion in TETD sensitized persons, it may rise to 0.2–0.4 mg. per cent or more.

As regards the metabolism of TETD, 90 per cent is absorbed from the intestine, it is detoxified in the liver and 50 per cent is excreted in twenty-four hours in urine mostly in a reduced form. One fifth remains in the body at the end of a week and thereafter is slowly excreted. Clinically, therefore, an attempt is made to saturate the body and then maintain the level by replacing the small amount excreted. One tablet (0.5 Gm.) is given daily, at bedtime. It is known that there is a lag of about twelve hours from the time of ingestion to a possible alcohol-TETD reaction probably due to the necessity of reduction of TETD in the body before it becomes active. A reaction is possible for four or five days after the drug is discontinued.

By itself TETD is relatively non-toxic in reasonable doses to both animals and man. It may occasionally cause acniform eruptions, lassi-ture, tremor and restlessness, decreased potency, dizziness and mild gastrointestinal symptoms. Drowsiness, probably the most common side effect, may be beneficial during recovery from acute intoxication, but patients must be advised of this possibility and due precautions taken to prevent accidents. Because of this, it is customary to prescribe the drug to be taken at night. Undesirable side effects may be lessened by reducing the dosage of TETD to one half tablet (0.25 Gm.) or one quarter tablet (0.125 Gm.). Psychotic reactions are likewise lessened with the smaller dosage.

The basis then of TETD therapy lies in the possibility of a reaction if and when alcohol is ingested. The reaction may occur in two phases, the first of which occurs five to fifteen minutes after drinking and as previously described includes widespread flushing over the face and upper extremities, injection of sclerae and conjunctiva, tachycardia, dyspnea, and hyperventilation. Subjective feelings are fright, restlessness, fear of impending death, and a feeling of chest constriction. These symptoms usually roughly parallel the amount of ingested alcohol. All this may precede a restful sleep at the end of one half hour or so, or it may be the prelude to a second, more dangerous, reaction from thirty to sixty minutes later. Though not consistently so, there is a greater likelihood of this delayed reaction with a greater amount of ingested alcohol. The vasodilation is followed by pallor and sweating together with nausea and vomiting. Blood pressure may fall rapidly and severe shock and coma may supervene causing severe problems because of cerebral and myocardial anoxia. EKG changes are frequent and convulsions have been reported. Patients on TETD should carry a card so stating with directions for the routine treatment to abort reactions: intravenous fluids, oxygen and shock position, ascorbic acid (500 mg., minimum), antihistamics (such as chlor-trimeton 100 mg.) are recommended. Because of the frequent insidious development of a delayed reaction, twenty-four hour hospital observation of a patient recovering from the alcohol-TETD reaction is recommended. The patient must be told that even after stopping medication the effect of TETD last for four days. TETD should not be administered until there have been at least four days of complete sobriety.

During the first few years of its use, drinking trials to induce a TETD reaction were customary. And for this patients were usually hospitalized. Fewer physicians are now precipitating planned alcohol-TETD reactions, since it is difficult to anticipate the severity of a reaction. A mild test reaction might make a patient feel reassured about future drinking with unfortunate later results and anxiety in relation to the unknown may well be an important deterrent. The results of drinking while sensitized should be made repeatedly clear to the patient and he should be warned of small unexpected sources of alcohol, such as wine cookery and cough medicine.

Selection of Patients

Before institution of therapy with TETD, there should be a thorough medical and psychiatric work-up including investigation of renal, hepatic and cardiac status. While there are no absolute clear-cut contra-indications, in each case the potential danger of the alcohol-TETD reaction must be considered within the frame of the patient's physical status, in relation to his motivation and to the severity of the alcohol problem and its prognosis. Coronary arterial heart disease, when present, greatly increases the hazard, since in the event of an alcohol-TETD reaction the coronary circulation is further decreased due to general vasodilation and various degrees of hypotension. There is need for careful evaluation of this risk compared to that involved in continued uncontrolled drinking. This applies also to liver impairment, diabetes mellitus, hyperthyroidism and epilepsy. There is evidence that diabetes mellitus may increase in severity with TETD and this should be watched for and proper measures taken to control it.

Diminished kidney function requires careful evaluation since a large part of the drug is excreted by that route. Caution also is needed with hyperthyroid patients. In epileptics increased frequency of convulsions has been reported. From a psychiatric standpoint the possibility of a breakdown of defenses in patients whose adjustment is marginal must be kept in mind and the use of TETD in latent psychotics should be carefully weighed. For, in some cases of latent psychoses, alcohol protects against an open psychotic episode. With some patients who are potentially psychotic, an overt psychotic episode may be contributed to by a toxic effect of the TETD itself. Support for this is found in the fact that when higher doses of TETD were used, as high as ten per cent of patients experienced these episodes. Since the dosage was reduced, they are rather rare. The commonest contraindication is probably lack of motivation. Its usefulness is greatest in patients with a well established conscious desire to be totally abstinent yet who find the impulse to drink at times uncontrollable. The unpleasant reality of the alcohol-TETD reaction helps many of these patients to avoid the first impulsive drink. It is also useful in keeping patients sober during the early phases of treatment until such time as they become more amenible to psychotherapy. Observations have shown that the more compulsive patients tend to do well on TETD since it provides the patient with a ritual and the taking of a pill becomes a routine procedure. Also it tends to decrease the patient's preoccupation with alcohol since when not on TETD he may have to face the decision whether to drink or not to drink a dozen times a day—when sensitized there is only one decision.

In summary, as experience has accumulated, it has become apparent that TETD is neither a cure-all nor the dangerous drug that its indiscriminate use in the earlier phases led many to believe. With careful screening of patients, smaller doses, and positive indications together with careful supervision of the patient, it offers a useful adjunct in the treatment of alcoholism.

OTHER TREATMENTS

In this section are included those treatment procedures that have been used effectively by some, but as yet have not received general support or sufficiently extensive trial. Others are included because of their interesting possibilities. And still others are discussed to be condemned as useless or harmful.

The AVERSION TREATMENT based on Pavlov's discovery of the conditioned reflex, Voegtlin,[9] Kant[5] and others. Voegtlin explains to the patient that the hypodermic injection which he receives will sensitize his nervous system so that the true obnoxious character of liquor will become more apparent to him. In the face of a battery of bottles filled with various types of liquor, wine and beer, the patient is given two 10 oz. glasses of warm saline solution containing one and one half grains of oral emetine and one gram of sodium chloride to the twenty ounces of water. Immediately after this six minims of a 40 c.c. sterile water solution containing 3.25 grams of emetine hydro-chloride to produce emesis, 1.65 grams of pilocarpine hydrochloride for diaphoresis and 1.5 grams of ephedrine sulphate is injected. From there on the patient is asked to drink whiskey—about 4 ounces—every ounce of whiskey in four ounces of luke warm water. The patient is told to sip it slowly, taste it thoroughly and swish it around in his mouth before he swallows it. Nausea should begin immediately after the second whiskey if the timing has been right. The first session is concluded by giving the patient a two ounce glass of near-beer to which tarter emetic is added for the purpose of prolonging the nausea. The first treatment is concluded after twenty minutes, and from five to eight treatments are usually given. Later treatments are prolonged up to thirty-five minutes. The amount of emetine injected is gradually increased to 15 minims and all types of alcoholic beverages are given in each treatment. If signs of liquor absorption appear and the patient begins to feel dizzy or gets a glow from the liquor, the stomach is immediately emptied by a tube to avoid intoxication. Psychotherapy is limited to a discussion of the patient's problem and an explanation of his susceptibilities to alcohol.

Kant has used a modification of this procedure. He emphasizes the fact that the patient who has undergone a well administered conditioned reflex treatment is immune to the temptation of drinking, at least for several months, and there has opened up much greater possibility for a psychotherapeutic approach outside of the hospital.

BARBITUATES, PARALDEHYDE, chloral-hydrate and hyacine have been used as chemotherapeutic means of treating alcoholics. While these medications are in some instances useful for short periods of time in acute states of alcoholism, their use over a prolonged period is to be condemned. It is well known that the alcoholic with his "addictive personality" can and usually does develop an addiction to drugs other than alcohol. Thus what may appear to be a cure of alcoholism simply represents a change from one type of addiction to another. Therefore narcotics are to be particularly condemned in the treatment of alcoholism since many an alcoholic has become a narcotic addict due to the use of narcotics in medical treatment. Rauwolfia, chlorpromazine and the newer tranquillizers do seem to be effective in the treatment of some cases of acute and chronic alcoholism, (see CHAPTER II) but it is still too early in the use of these medications for a clear-cut evaluation to have been established. On the other hand, it should be noted that cases of addiction to the tranquilizers have been observed.

THE VITAMINS, particularly the B-complex group are extremely important in the treatment of the medical and neuropsychiatric complications of alcoholism. (See CHAPTERS III and IV.) It is felt by some that deficiencies of certain vitamin components, such as pantothenic acid, pyrixidyne, niacin and riboflavin may be basic causes of the alcoholic's need to drink. On the basis of this, various treatment programs have been devised using these components, and especially thiamine, as a means of treating the addiction to alcohol itself. Most observers, however, are of the opinion that vitamin deficiencies are secondary to the drinking. While it is true that an injection of intraveneous thiamine chloride will give the patient a temporary "lift," there is no convincing experimental or theoretical data to indicate that it is a useful procedure nor are the results of such treatment at all convincing.

Smith [8] and Lovell and Tintera [6] reported on the use of ADRENAL CORTICAL EXTRACTS (ACE) and adrenal cortical trophic-hormone (ACTH). These endocrine products have been especially useful in the acute alcoholic states, but not for chronic alcoholism. They have reported on the value of the use of these preparations with patients who have a syndrome of hypoglycemia, low 17-ketosteroids, and low androgens. It is felt that a low tolerance to alcohol is correlated with this syndrome of hypoadrenocorticism. ACTH, in a dosage of 25 i.u. intramuscularly every six hours, is reported by some to be the most effective treatment for delirium tremens. According to Selye [7] worry, grief and alarm stimuli together with alcohol, produce hyperthrophy of the adrenal cortex with eventual hypoadrenocorticism which may be benefitted by the use of ACE. Smith recommends the use of a 100 to 150 milligrams of ACTH intramuscularly in divided doses over a twenty-five to thirty-six hour period. If ACTH is not available ACE can be substituted.

The consensus is that alcoholism in itself does not indicate ELECTRIC SHOCK THERAPY. The chief indications for use of electric shock in alcoholic patients are where alcoholism is secondary to functional psychoses (schizophrenia, manic-depressive reactions and especially involutional psychosis). Because alcoholism is sometimes the presenting symptom in these disorders, the underlying dysfunction which is treatable by electric shock may be obscured.

In the CARBON DIOXIDE INHALATION method of treatment, the patient inhales carbon dioxide to the point of unconsciousness.[2, 4] Treatments are given three to five times a week for forty or fifty treatments and then continued with lesser frequency for maintenance. More recent evaluations indicate this procedure may have limited usefulness. When it is effective it appears to be so in some alcoholics with marked, overt anxiety, however, in such patients the effect is also unpredictable.

REFERENCES

1. FELDMAN, D. J.: Drug therapy of chronic alcoholism. Med. Cl. N. Am. *41:* 381, 1957.
2. FRANK, J. A.: Critical evaluation of carbon dioxide—oxygen inhalation therapy in mental disorders. Am. J. Psych. *110:* 93, Aug. 1953.

3. HALD, J., AND JACOBSEN, E.: A drug sensitizing the organism to ethyl alcohol. Lancet. *255:* 1001, 1948.
4. HERMAN, M.: Personal Communication.
5. KANT, F.: The Treatment of the Alcoholic. Springfield, Charles C Thomas, 1954.
6. LOVELL, H., AND TINTERA, J.: Endocrine treatment of alcoholism. Geriatrics, Sept.–Oct., 1949.
7. SELYE, H. J.: Diseases of the Adrenals. Montreal, Univ. Montreal Press, 1946.
8. SMITH, J. J.: Endocrine basis and hormonal therapy of alcoholism. New York State J. Med. *50:* 1704–1706, July 15, 1950.
9. VOEGTLIN, W. C.: The treatment of alcoholism by establishing a conditioned reflex. Am. J. M. Sc. *199:* 804–809, 1940.

VII   *The Consolidated Edison-*
New York University-
Bellevue Medical Center Plan

ON THE following pages is described in detail the plan used by the Consolidated Edison Company of New York in collaboration with the New York University-Bellevue Medical Center in the treatment of alcoholics. To the author's knowledge, this is the most intensively developed plan and is the one with which he is familiar from first-hand experiences. It is hoped that some or all of the aspects of this particular plan will be useful in application to other industries.

COMPANY PROCEDURE [1]

In 1947 the Consolidated Edison Company of New York, Inc. officially recognized chronic alcoholism as a medical condition and adopted a "Company Procedure on Alcoholism." This decision was based on a policy of meeting the problem openly instead of perpetuating the outworn pretense that it did not exist. The aim of the procedure was threefold: (1) The early recognition of the employee with a drinking problem, (2) rehabilitation of the employee if possible, and (3) the establishment of a consistent basis for termination of employment when attempts at rehabilitation failed.

The first step in this program was an interview with the employee's immediate supervisor, usually in the presence of the union shop steward. After the employee was placed on probation, he was referred to the medical department where an examination was carried out. The prime purpose of this examination was classification of the chronic problem drinkers, and in particular cases, the services of a psychiatrist were enlisted. Efforts were made toward psychological adjustment with help by the company in solving financial problems or facilitating job reassignment. Domestic situations were more difficult to handle, but aid was offered to the employee in terms of "reorienting his attitudes." Distinct benefits were derived from this program, but in May 1951 the late Dr. John J. Wittmer proposed a plan of treatment and rehabilitation of alcoholics in industry to be carried out in a special center outside of the company setting. In January 1952 Consolidated Edison volunteered to underwrite the cost of the Consultation Clinic for Alcoholism at the University Hospital of the New York University-Bellevue Medical Center. The clinic, the first to be devoted solely to the alcoholic in industry, was formally opened on February 4, 1952.

Administration of the Procedure

Under the Company Procedure of the Consolidated Edison Company, the foreman and supervisor have the responsibility for the recognition of the early signs of uncontrolled use of alcohol among men working under them. It is not the responsibility of the medical department to discover alcoholics, but the industrial medical department does have a role to play in the early recognition of the drinking problem which is masquerading as a medical illness. The medical department has the responsibility for diagnosis and for supervision of medical rehabilitation.

A training program for supervisors and foremen is in continuous operation to instruct this group in the understanding of the objectives of the "Company Procedure on Alcoholism" and to assist them in recognizing the early signs of problem drinking.

At the company it was recognized that the following signs are indicative of the early phase of a drinking problem, and often characteristic of the alcoholic "hidden man."

1. Consistent tardiness or absence on Monday morning and frequent occurrences of leaving early on Friday afternoon.
2. Unexplained disappearance from an assigned post during a tour of duty.
3. Recurrent excuses for absence due to minor illnesses or too-frequent off-duty accidents, particularly with assault as a factor.
4. Personality change in a previously good worker; such as arguments with others, recurrent mistakes for which he defends himself, minor accidents which he blames on others or on equipment, marked variation in mood and disinterest in his work.

Operation of the Company Procedure

The basis of the "Company Procedure on Alcoholism" is the use of a firm, judicious probation policy. This has been coupled with an adequate medical facility for rehabilitation. Probation is tentatively set at one year, with the understanding that it is really for an indefinite period. Since the employee may be denied progression increases, depending on his length of service, during the period of probation, the company limits probation to one year to provide an incentive for his rehabilitation and a reward for his efforts. It would be poor psychology to extend this period officially. However, any relapse after the one year period still brings the employee under immediate review by the panel as described below.

The steps in the operation of the "Procedure on Alcoholism" are described as follows:

WHEN ANY department of the company is confronted with a behavior problem arising from repeated alcoholic excess, the employee is given a preliminary warning by his immediate supervisor. This warning is always incorporated in the employee's record. In some instances we have observed that the warning may be repeated several times before definitive action is taken.

WHEN THERE is a recurrence of the drinking situation, the employee is immediately interviewed by his supervisor and placed on probation. In the event of a serious drinking situation, such as being found drunk on an operating job or an extended bender or hospitalization, the individual may be promptly placed on probation without undergoing any preliminary warning. In such cases, a review of the employee's record often brings out other facts of significance, such as repeated absences or instances suspicious of overindulgence on the job. The employee can request the shop steward to be present at the interview and this is often the case. Over the years, a feeling of mutual trust has developed between the union and management on the handling of drinking problems since the goal of the company procedure has been to give the employee a chance to rehabilitate himself.

The department head notifies the personnel director and furnishes him with a written report of all the circumstances to be forwarded to the medical department. Experience indicates that a complete and detailed report giving the entire story is of tremendous assistance to the physician in making his evaluation of the case. The employee in his interview with his immediate supervisor is advised that information he conveys to the examining physician may not be considered as a privileged communication.

THE MEDICAL department has the responsibility of determining if the employee is, in fact, an alcoholic and of estimating the extent of his illness. If the medical department confirms that the employee has a drinking problem, he is offered the opportunity for rehabilitation through the Consultation Clinic for Alcoholism at the University Hospital. On the other hand, the employee may choose to report to A. A. or place himself under the care of his own physician or even refuse to follow any recommended treatment.

Upon completion of the examination, a brief medical report is forwarded to the department head which indicates that the individual fits into one of four categories: not an alcoholic, questionable alcoholic, alcoholic or chronic alcoholic. The term "questionable alcoholic" usually covers the occasional excessive symptomatic drinker or the alcoholic where the paucity of facts at hand prevents the formation of a definite diagnosis. This term may also be used when a neuropsychiatric condition is dominant and it is questionable if a drinking problem per se is present.

IF THE drinking offense recurs, the employee is immediately suspended by his department and a panel for adjudication of his case is convened at the earliest possible moment. This panel includes a representative of management, the personnel and medical departments and the department which employs the individual. The employee is reexamined and at this stage the medical department report is detailed and conveys medical information that might in other circumstances be considered confidential. As noted above, the employee has previously been advised that information he conveys to the examining physician may be revealed at the panel discussion of his problem. In actual practice this has proven of great value to the employee concerned because it allows the medical department to present the train of circumstances which caused the relapse. Extenuating circumstances are considered by the department.

At the panel, after all information has been presented and evaluated, the department renders its decision. This is discussed and reviewed by the whole panel. While alcoholism is treated as a medical condition, it gets no disproportionate share of attention. Means are provided to discipline and even discharge the occasional offender whose problem does not seem to be related to any underlying psychological or medical situation. With the worthwhile results of the company program, the number of cases that have required panel review has decreased over the years.

Final action is determined in accordance with established procedure as follows:

(a) There is no medical or psychological basis for the drinking condition; action is to be determined by the employee's department. This obtains when the employee has been classified as "not an alcoholic." Departmental action in these conditions can result in discharge.

(b) There is an underlying disease resulting from chronic alcoholism and the prognosis is poor. The employee is recommended for the disability roll, but he does not receive the customary sick allowances as obtains in the case of purely medical disability.

(c) There is an underlying disease, but the prognosis is good as in certain cases of cirrhosis of the liver and peripheral neuritis. The employee may be placed on the sick roll and receives sick allowances during such rehabilitation.

(d) The case is one of chronic or psychopathic alcoholism. The employee is then recommended for the disability roll without the benefit of preceding sick allowances.

A brief word about the relationship to the Consultation Clinic. Every effort is made to reassure the employee that the clinic functions separately from the company. Policy with respect to the Consultation Clinic can be summarized as covering the following four points:

1. The patient is referred only by the medical department and, of course, always with his consent. The largest group comprises those coming under the company procedure. The second group consists of those employees who have a medical condition in which alcoholism is considered to be a contributory factor. Finally, there are those employees who voluntarily present themselves because of a drinking problem.

2. The confidential nature of the doctor-patient relationship at the clinic is maintained. No reports are transmitted from the clinic to the medical department.

3. The employee pays the cost of his own clinic visits.

4. Hospitalization is at the individual's own expense. It should be noted that only one employee required short term hospitalization for initiation of treatment.

SUMMARY

A definitive company policy is the first step toward a program for meeting the situation of problem drinking in industry. To begin with, it proclaims management's interest and support. It is essential that a complete understanding and an unreserved acceptance of the company program be obtained at all levels of management. This is best achieved by a forthright acknowledgement of top management that the problem really exists. A well defined company policy should form the practical basis for administrative procedures to cover (1) early recognition, (2) rehabilitation, and (3) a consistent method for termination of employment when efforts to effect rehabilitation are unsuccessful.

The second step in the program is the establishment of medical facilities for rehabilitation. Without adequate means for treatment, a company program may degenerate into mere disciplinary measures. Success or failure of a company program will depend largely on the industrial physician's ability to locate and develop resources for treatment.

When adequate attempts at rehabilitation of an employee have failed, the termination of his employment on a consistent basis is usually necessary in the interest of good personnel procedures. From a practical point of view, the success of a company program will sharply reduce the need for termination measures.

The ultimate goal of any company procedure is the prevention of the disability from chronic problem drinking. A well conceived and directed program is a firm step in this direction. The good results of industrial programs actually in operation indicate that such efforts not only yield material rewards in salvaging the skill and experience of long service employees, but also contribute to an over-all improvement in employee relations.

THE UNIVERSITY CLINIC FOR ALCOHOLISM [5]

It is the purpose of this section to present a description of the Consultation Clinic for Alcoholism which functions in collaboration with the Consolidated Edison Company of New York (see preceding and following sections). The aspects to be presented include the administrative arrangements, referral processes, diagnostic and treatment procedures and impressions of special features of the problem drinker, and implications of the use of probation.

Administrative Arrangement

The Consultation Clinic for Alcoholism is one of several specialty clinics in the Department of Psychiatry of the New York University College of Medicine, and is also under the supervision of the Department of Industrial Medicine of the New York University Post-Graduate Medical School. The clinic is located in the University Hospital where laboratory, hospital and consultation services are available. The two medical schools and the hospital are units of the New York University-Bellevue Medical Center.

TABLE 1. ADMINISTRATIVE ARRANGEMENT

Position	Time Devoted (Hours per week)	Duties
Psychiatrist	20	Project supervisor, initial screening, psychotherapy, group and individual.
Psychiatrist	3	Individual and group psychotherapy.
Psychiatrist	6	Individual and group psychotherapy.
Psychiatrist	3	Group psychotherapy.
Internist	6	Initial medical survey, treatment of related medical problems.
Psychologist	30	Psychological evaluation, research assistant.
Secretary	40	

The personnel of the clinic consists of psychiatrists, psychologists and an internist. Each member receives a stipend and devotes a fixed amount of time to the clinic. The original administrative arrangement is presented in TABLE 1.

Subsequent and minor changes have taken place with respect to personnel and allotted time; the specific duties remain as stated. More recently, a research psychologist has been added to the staff. When necessary the clinic makes use of the social work department of the University Hospital. Selection of personnel depends upon such factors as availability of trained workers and funds for hiring them, so that the administrative composition of Consultation Clinic represents just one of several suitable arrangements.

The above approach is an important means of stimulating the inter-change of ideas regarding individual patients and the problem of al-coholism in general. It also facilitates a multi-disciplined approach to the diagnostic and treatment phases of each patient.

To enhance individual contributions to the overall functioning of the clinic, seminars are held once a week. These meetings are devoted to presentation of case material, theoretical discussions, and critical evaluation of new techniques for treating the alcoholic patient.

Although the main attention of the clinic is focused on the treatment of the alcoholic patient, a research orientation pervades all functions. It has been found that such an orientation is valuable in not only pro-viding much needed scientific information in the field of alcoholism but also in attracting highly trained personnel, and sustaining a clinic atmosphere of enthusiasm and vitality.

Clinic Procedure

Fourteen companies * have utilized the services of the Consultation Clinic for Alcoholism by paying a consultation fee for the initial evaluation of their employees. Treatment offered to the employee fol-lowing this evaluation period is charged to the individual on a regular clinic fee basis. The probationary system, under which the employee is referred, varies from company to company, with the most definitive and extensive procedure followed by the Consolidated Edison Company of New York (see preceding section). At that company the employee is referred, with his consent, through the medical department. Con-solidated Edison Company classified the three types of patients whom they send to the clinic as one, those coming under Company Procedure; two, those not under the "Company Alcohol Procedure" in whom al-coholism is considered by the medical department physician as a con-tributory factor in a medical problem; three, those employees who voluntarily come to the clinic because they realize their drinking is causing a problem in some phase of life, though not as yet interfering with job performance.

* American Brake Shoe Company, American Can Company, Bell Telephone Laboratories, Beta Electronic Corporation, Equitable Life Assurance Company, Esso Shipping Company, Johns-Manville Corporation, Metropolitan Life Insurance Company, New York Telephone Company, The New York Times, Ohrbachs and Sperry Gyroscope. (Consolidated Edison Company of New York and Standard Oil of New Jersey have a different financial arrangement.)

EACH PATIENT is seen initially by the psychiatrist in charge of the clinic for one or more sessions. Important goals of these interviews are to establish good rapport with the patient, to dissuade him from his conception of the clinic as an extension of his company, and to elicit more positive motivation for treatment. An overall evaluation is also made of the drinking problem in the physical, emotional, social, family and vocational areas. Finally, on the basis of the above data and clinical impressions a determination is made concerning which of the several treatments, either singly or in combination, is best suited for the particular patient (see TABLE 2).

TABLE 2. REFERRAL AND CLINIC PROCEDURE

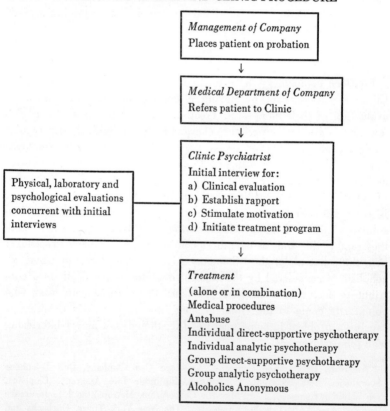

CONCURRENT WITH the initial interviews, the patient has physical, laboratory (complete blood count, serology, urine and chest x-ray)

and psychological (Bellevue-Wechsler, Rorschach, Thematic Appercep-
tion Test) examinations. These examinations are scheduled to take
place on the same or closely ensuing days in order to shorten the
work-up period. Our experience indicates that such examinations
should be carried out expeditiously in order to launch the patient into
treatment as quickly as possible. Increased clinical judgment has facilitated our reaching decisions concerning appropriate therapies. In those
instances where it had become apparent that the evaluations were incorrect, appropriate changes in the treatment program were made. In
most instances, psychological testing is delayed for several weeks because these patients may be still suffering from the effects of recent
drinking which could adversely influence the test results.

Treatment

Treatment consists mainly of individual psychotherapy, group psychotherapy, both directive-supportive and analytic; Antabuse, sedatives
and tranquilizers and in some instances referral to Alcoholics Anonymous (see CHAPTER V).

Hospitalization for acute alcoholism or post-alcoholic states has
been surprisingly rare in the industrial patients studied and treated.
The large majority of these patients seen in an acute drinking state or
immediately thereafter are able to stop their drinking on an ambulatory
regimen. During this period they are seen frequently by psychiatrist
and internist and given appropriate medication. Those few patients who
require hospitalization are individuals in whom study and evaluation
reveal a poor prognosis for achieving abstinence on an ambulatory
basis or where subsequent course indicated this. With the patient who
is sufficiently motivated even the occurrence of an acute crisis of a
bout of uncontrolled drinking can be successfully handled in the clinic.

Hospitalization for conditions other than those directly related to
alcoholism are not undertaken by the clinic staff, but managed by a
private physician or the company medical department. In such instances,
a member of the clinic staff maintains liaison with the attending
physician.

PROBATION AND MOTIVATION

It is the observation of most experienced workers in the field of
alcoholism that the alcoholic can not be helped irrespective of the
particular therapeutic approach unless he is motivated toward treatment

or has the capacity for developing such motivation. The alcoholic usually makes extensive use of the mechanism of denial—the unconscious refuation of painful realities—which in this case includes the drinking problem and the devastations of alcoholism. Usually he must undergo some serious, meaningful personal loss or impairment before there is relinquishing of the denial mechanism. Because of the extensiveness of the denial system and the consequent lack of realization of problems, the alcoholic patient usually seeks help of his own accord only when the driking already has eventuated in marked physical, mental, vocational, or family losses.

The patients referred by industry, however, have not for the most part reached this terminal stage of alcoholism with its widespread disruption of functions. As such, they have not become aware of the seriousness of their present status or the likelihood of future disaster. It is at this point that the judicious application of company probation plays an important role in providing the employee with reasonably good motivation for treatment at the clinic. This does not mean to infer that all patients referred to us by industry come to the clinic happily and enthusiastically. Not infrequently, in the first session the patient may be resentful toward the company for placing him on probation, and he may speak of the unfairness of it. He also may be extremely resentful toward the clinic, since he knows that his company has contributed financially to the clinic and, therefore, regards the clinic as an extension of the disciplinarian company. In dealing with this problem, we try to dissipate the resentful attitudes toward the clinic by reassuring the patient that the clinic functions quite separately from the company. The patient is told that nothing he says or does will be reported to the company and under no circumstances can they obtain any of his records without his written permission.

It is extraordinary to see how the drinking itself is managed by these patients either prior to coming to the clinic and immediately after being put on probation or after an initial session or two at the clinic. In the vast majority of cases, the drinking stops completely. The factor of probation in the special group of patients seen at the clinic has many psychological implications. In essence, the alcoholic in industry has been warned on one or more occasions about his drinking. He is finally put on probation with the clear understanding that should drinking occur again he will lose his job. This threat is extremely effective in motivating the desire for help because of the importance work has for this group of alcoholics. The average period of employment at the same company is 22 years. This statistic itself is indicative of the importance of the job to the patient. Usually, it is a question of not only salary, medical care, and pension advantages but also long established emotional ties to other employees, supervisors, and the company. The threat of loss of all this touches on areas that have genuine meaning for these patients, and, almost without exception, one sees the balance of forces turned in the direction of strong motivation for abstinence from alcohol.

RESULTS OF THE CONSOLIDATED EDISON-NEW YORK UNIVERSITY-BELLEVUE PLAN

Two follow-up studies have been made to evaluate the results of the Consolidated Edison-New York University-Bellevue Plan; one study was conducted at the Consultation Clinic for Alcoholism,[6] the other at the Consolidated Edison Company.[1]

During the years 1952 to 1955 inclusive, 183 cases of alcoholism were recognized at the Consolidated Edison Company. Of these, the vast majority of cases (147) were recognized under the "Company Procedure on Alcoholism." (See preceding section.) The diagnosis of alcoholism was made in the course of medical examination in the cases of 27 employees and 9 employees volunteered for treatment for alcoholism. Review of the age and service of the 183 employees indicates that alcoholism became evident mainly between 46 and 54 years of age when the average number of years of service was over twenty.

Of the 183 cases reviewed at Consolidated Edison 145 accepted referral to the Consultation Clinic. Twenty-six employees refused treatment at the clinic and were followed only in the medical department of the company. Twelve employees were not referred. Four of these 12 were questionable alcoholics; three employees had clear-cut psychiatric disorders with drinking an incidental manifestation. The remaining five employees who were not referred to the clinc were advanced alcoholics with marked and irreversible organic deterioration.

As indicated in TABLE 3, of the 145 employees referred to the clinic, 93 (64 per cent) were able to keep their jobs. However, 72 per cent of those who continued treatment at the clinic maintained their jobs; only 45 per cent of those who discontinued treatment at the clinic after initial interviews were able to keep their jobs.

Of the 26 employees who refused treatment at the clinic, 16 (61 per cent) kept their jobs. More detailed evaluation of the treatment results can be visualized in a review of the recovery scale of these 183 employees. Of those who continued treatment at the clinic over 60 per cent are considered rehabilitated or socially recovered and 30 per cent are much improved. By contrast, while 61 per cent of those who refused treatment at the Consultation Clinic were also able to maintain their jobs, only 25 per cent have made real progress toward recovery and rehabilitation. The poor results among those who discontinued treatment were made worse by the addition of those who relapsed within the first few months of treatment and discontinued therapy at the clinic when their employment was terminated.

Of the twelve employees who were not referred to the clinic, only two maintained their jobs; these were two of the four employees for whom the diagnosis of alcoholism was questionable. The other two were discharged. The three employees with psychiatric disorders and the five with organic deterioration due to alcohol had termination of their employment either by separation allowance or disability retirement.

Scrutiny of the period of observation indicates that over 60 per cent of those who lost their jobs did so within the first year of follow-up. Relapse of the drinking episode poses a very serious problem. In the early years of our experience, panel review of such cases usually led to termination of employment on some basis. After the establishment of the Consultation Clinic there developed the philosophy that if an individual made a real effort toward rehabilitation at the clinic and nevertheless suffered a relapse in the first three to four months of treatment, the employee could be given another opportunity at rehabilitation measures. Likewise, a relapse even after one year or more of treatment in an employee who had made sincere efforts to help himslf did not prejudice a further trial at rehabilitation. Of the seventy-two employees who continued treatment at the clinic there were eight who suffered relapses after intervals varying from one to three years.

The evaluation, by the operating departments, of the progress of the employees under the "Procedure on Alcoholism" approximated the medical department's evaluation of progress. In September 1955, 86 cases whose medical follow-up results had been listed as good in 71 and poor in 15 were reviewed by their own departments in reference to general attitude and work performance. By January 31, 1956 the departments' opinions were rendered as follows: 58 good progress, 17 fair progress, 6 poor results (terminated or being terminated under

TABLE 3. FOLLOW-UP STUDY

ALCOHOLISM PROGRAM: 1952–1955

Method of Treatment	Total	Maintained Jobs	Lost Jobs
1. Referred to Clinic	145	93 (64%)	52
a. Continued Treatment	99	72 (72%)	27
b. Discontinued Treatment or Terminated within 6 months	46	21 (45%)	25
2. Refused Treatment at Clinic	26	16 (61%)	10
3. Not Referred to Clinic	12	2	10
	183	111 (60%)	72

RECOVERY SCALE OF EMPLOYEES WHO MAINTAINED JOBS

	Continued Clinic Treatment	Discontinued Clinic Treatment	Refused Clinic Treatment
Rehabilitated	29.3%		12.4%
Socially Recovered	34 %	9.5%	12.4%
Much Improved	30 %	23.8%	37.4%
Somewhat Improved	4 %	38.2%	6.6%
Unimproved	2.7%	28.5%	31.2%

Period of Observation	Total	Maintained Jobs	Lost Jobs
Less than 12 months	46		46
12–18 months	33	21	12
19–24 months	19	13	6
25–36 months	38	33	5
37–48 months	30	27	3
49–60 months	17	17	

NOTE: 1948–1951, (prior to use of special clinic) Total—145 cases, 61 (42%) maintained jobs.

the "Procedure on Alcoholism"), and 5 were retired for either age or other causes not related to alcoholism.

Analysis of the method of termination of those employees who lost their jobs revealed that thirty cases received disability annuities and twenty were granted allowances limited as to duration. Three were considered medically disabled because of a dominant psychiatric condition. Three employees died of chronic alcoholic disease. To illustrate that the alcoholism procedure was not intended as a reward for misbehavior, ten cases were discharged and six resigned.

Another tangible result of the company program on alcoholism has been the reduction in absenteeism in the cases involved. The average recorded sick absence in the Consultation Clinic cases for a three year period prior to referral was 13.5 days per year, approximately double the company average. We have reason to believe that absence due to alcoholic episodes may have been as much as three times the average because many of the absences under review were masked as medical conditions. Since the inception of treatment, the absence severity rate has been less than four days per year in the rehabilitated cases.

THE RECOVERED ALCOHOLIC

The alcoholic who has achieved abstinence from alcohol by virtue of this fact alone and regardless of the means used shows remarkable improvement in all areas of adaptation. To begin with, he looks and reacts in a healthier way; the "bloated" effect of the face disappears. General physical condition improves and most of the physical complications of alcoholism disappear or improve. For example, morning vomiting disappears, sleep may initially be worsened and a cause for great complaint, but gradually sleep improves over a period of weeks or months. Appetite returns, there is usually weight gain. Many of the psychiatric symptoms disappear, for example, shakiness, phobias, fears of insanity and seclusiveness. Paranoid features are markedly lessened and it is now possible to make better contact with the patient. Subjectively there is marked improvement. The patient enjoys his sobriety and looks back with horror at what he has been through. Retrospectively he may regard his drinking and behavior as foolish or "crazy." He is often appreciative towards those who forced him to seek help and perhaps expresses the wish that it had occurred sooner. Interest and involvement with job, family, friends and hobbies increase. In a word, the patient is quite different.

In accounting for these marked changes, one may point first to the elimination of the direct toxic effects of alcohol. Also, there are the improved eating habits, more regular hours and in general getting back into a more reasonable routine. From a psychological point of view, the changes are enormous. There is a reversal of all the psychological consequences of drinking. Now perception is clearer. More distinction is made between outer reality and subjective experiences, between fact and fantasy. The patient's capacity for judgment and delay of action are increased. Wishful thinking is progressively replaced by more realistic thinking and various interests and hobbies previously dissolved by alcohol are now reinstituted. The patient's energies are now under the sway of a more regulated economy, as opposed to the previous chaos. The patient sees himself more realistically. Relations with people are re-established. The patient comes out of a dream world into a world of reality. These psychological improvements naturally evidence themselves most vividly to those closest to the alcoholic, especially family and supervisor at work who has a good opportunity to observe the employee in his work effectiveness and in his relations with other workers. It is striking to see how close is the correlation of opinions regarding improvement between the employee's therapist at the clinic and the employee's supervisor, demonstrating the close connection between the patient's psychic functioning and its manifestations in the practical work area.

In summary, a consistent company alcohol procedure combined with a special clinic for the treatment of alcoholics has eventuated in excellent results. Sixty-four per cent of those referred to the clinic were able to maintain their jobs. Seventy-two per cent of those who continued in treatment maintained their jobs. Absenteeism for this group of alcoholics was reduced from an average of 13.5 days per year to less than 4 days per year. Aside from these factors which more readily lend themselves to statistical analysis, there are the less tangible results of increased work efficiency and improved relations among employees. There are savings in separation allowances and retirement pay and the special addition to company pride and morale in having made an important contribution to salvaging of employees and having contributed to medical knowledge in assisting in clarifying new means of motivating alcoholics to seek help.

It must be emphasized that the high incidence of recovery in this particular group of alcoholics in industry does not necessarily reflect on the possibilities for comparable recovery rates in alcoholics in general. This group of alcoholics is specially selected and specially motivated. The long tenure of job (average of twenty years) reflects on good job stability which in turn is indicative of personal strengths and potentialities. In relation to this fact, the realistic difficulties in obtaining other jobs in the older age groups and the various medical and retirement benefits the application of pressure in the form of threat of loss of job represents a unique and happy combination of circumstances.

SOME BRIEF CASE HISTORIES

Case 1: The Alcoholic Who Denies the Problem of Drinking

The patient is a 42 year old married man who has worked for his company for twenty-one years. For a period of two or three years, his absences from work showed a steady and marked increase so that he had come to the attention of the company physician. At the Consultation Clinic for Alcoholism, the patient protested that he had no idea why he had been referred. He asked the doctor why he had been referred to the clinic and was not only surprised but somewhat insulted when told that he was considered to have a problem with controlling his drinking. The patient initially insisted that he drank in amounts no greater than the people he knew both at work and away from work, that his control over drinking was more than adequate and that in no wise did alcohol have any deleterious effect upon any area in his life. As this patient talked about his work and his home life and his activities away from work, it soon became clearer that relationships with his wife and children were particularly strained, that he had been spoken to about the quality of his work at the company and had in fact missed out on a promotion—all in relation to excessive drinking. Much of his spare time was devoted to drinking with his friends in the local tavern.

Pointing these facts out to the patient resulted in the patient's reacting with indignation. Initially it was truthfully impossible for the patient to believe that he had a drinking problem which was interfering with his functioning at work and at home.

This patient was seen three times a week in directive-supportive individual psychotherapy at the Consultation Clinic. The main objective at the onset of this treatment was to break through this patient's defense of denial and to enable him to become aware of the extent to which drinking had involved the various phases of his life. This patient gradually began to perceive the therapist as a non-threatening person who was more interested in helping him rather than in condemning him for his drinking. Subsequently, the patient was willing to try to cut down on the amount of his drinking, largely out of pleasing the doctor, whom he now regarded as his friend rather than because of seeing any real necessity on his own. However, he soon realized that he was not able to simply diminish the amount of drinking nor was he able to do without drink. This became the first time the patient gained any awareness into the effect that drinking had upon him, and it was only as he continued his efforts to stop drinking that he became more and more concerned about its hold over him. At the same time the patient was able to see more clearly into his relationships with his wife and children at home, and as he became more concerned over the difficulties at home it was possible to discuss this area in the treatment. He also was able to speak about some of his feelings at work where resentments and frustration had previously been covered up by excessive drinking.

Ostensibly what happened in this case was an undoing of the defense of denial which was replaced by considerable anxiety and tension. This anxiety and tension was an important factor in motivating the patient to then deal with some of his psychological problems in terms of his relationships with other people and his ability to deal with himself. As he gained more strength to deal in a more forthright manner with feelings of tension and frustration without resorting to drinking, he became better able to overcome some of his problems. At the same time, by controlling his drinking he was able to establish a better relationship with his wife and children. The patient has been able to maintain a good level of functioning in all areas of life for the past year and one half without having to resort to drinking. Undoubtedly this patient would not have sought treatment voluntarily. It was only the fact of job probation that enabled him to make the initial step in seeking assistance.

Case 2: The Helpless Patient

This patient is a 38 year old single woman who had been employed by her company for seventeen years. She was referred to the clinic by the company doctor partly because the company felt that her drinking was interfering with her work and partly at the patient's own request. This patient cheerfully explained at the clinic that she suddenly became aware of her inability to control her drinking and that she was terribly ashamed of having to confess to such a lack of moral substance in herself. She was filled with self-recriminations and recognized the seriousness of her problem. She agreed with all that the company physician had told her and in fact went further in foreseeing a bleak end for herself. She felt, however, that the immensity of the problem was so overwhelming that she was helpless to deal with it or to even consider it in a constructive light. In a sense she threw herself upon the mercy of the physician and hoped that he, out of some degree of compassion, would make things all right for her.

The submissive, helpless way in which this patient presented her problem became one of the initial focal points in the psychotherapeutic treatment at the clinic. It had to be made clear to the patient that she was not helpless to do anything about her problem, that she was not a little child who had to be helped by the adults, but rather that she herself was an adult and was potentially capable of dealing with her drinking problem in an adult way. Such an approach of course aimed directly at her all-pervasive self-depreciatory attitudes toward herself. It was only as she was able to begin to regard herself in a more positive light that she was able to actively consider doing something constructive about her inability to control excessive drinking. It was at this point that she requested help in her first attempt to cut down on drinking; this patient was placed on Antabuse and started in group psychotherapy. The taking of Antabuse by this patient did not entirely play into her helplessness but rather it was regarded by her as her first positive act in stopping her drinking. She prided herself on not failing to take the Antabuse and soon began to enjoy the pleasure of being able to act on her own behalf—in her own behalf. Because of this and group psychotherapy, she felt strengthened and took courage to enter into relationships with the other girls at the company and was surprised to find how easily they accepted her. The patient's next step was to permit herself to enter into some superficial relationships with male companions both at the company and outside. In the last stages of this patient's reorientation toward herself, she was able to move out of her parents' home and to furnish her own apartment. This development coincided with the patient's re-evaluation of herself as an attractive, acceptable grown-up person who had a right to happiness in her own behalf and who did not have to surrender herself to the needs and demands of others.

Case 3: The "Strong" Patient

This patient is a 52 year old man, married and with two children. He had a relatively high level job at his company where he has worked for twenty-three years. The patient came to the clinic in a very forthright, active, well controlled manner indicating that he had been told by the company that his drinking problem was interfering with his work. He felt that he was "man enough to see the correctness of their evaluation and that he also was man enough to stop the drinking for-ever." In fact, this patient had stopped drinking the day before he reported to the Consultation Clinic and would not permit himself to allow for any craving or discomfort resulting from the giving up of drinking. This attitude pervaded almost all of his functioning wherein he felt that while there had been some difficulties in his relationship with his wife, these probably could be attributed to drinking and that he would rectify both problems by not drinking anymore. This also held true for his altercations with his children and with some disagree-ments with a supervisor at work.

The treatment at the Consultation Clinic with this patient was to encourage his self-made decisions and at the same time to help him see that there was no shame in requesting the help of someone else in his attempts to stop drinking. However, in this patient's case he never could accept the fact that he might need help from someone else, which he regarded as a sign of weakness. He continued along on his own, taking pleasure in the fact that he was strong enough to give up drinking all on his own. In truth, this patient managed very well to get along without drinking and did improve in his relationships both at work and at home. His visits to the clinic were increasingly infre-quent and spaced at increasingly longer periods of time. This was in accord with the patient's desires and psychological needs and permitted him to function without drinking for almost one year as of this date.

Case 4: An Emotionally Disturbed Patient Who Also Drank

This is the case of a 34 year old divorced man who was referred by his company for excessive drinking which interfered with his attendance at work and which apparently aggravated some physical difficulties in visual activities and co-ordination. This patient readily admitted to drinking but said that he felt that this was not his real problem; rather, that he had many psychological problems and drank only to relieve the tremendous tension under which he labored. This patient unfolded a life long history of emotional difficulties. He apparently has been for a number of years very tense and anxious, easily irritated and prone to periods of depression. He had found that drinking temporarily assuaged these pathological emotions but he had begun to rely to an ever increasing extent upon the help which alcohol afforded him.

This patient was very anxious to cooperate with the doctor in dealing with his psychological problems. It soon became apparent that the major problem for this patient was his deep seated emotional difficulties in which the drinking problem was of a secondary nature. While his treatment at the clinic afforded him some relief from tension, as did his receiving a tranquilizing drug, it was felt that this patient was in need of more intensive treatment than could be afforded at the clinic. It was also felt that this patient would be able to benefit from such treatment. Provisions were made so that this patient was referred to a psychoanalyst where he embarked on a rather intensive therapeutic course to resolve his psychological difficulties.

This is a case where it was very important to evaluate the true role of the alcoholism. In fact, it had been decided that the giving up of alcohol in this patient before the resolution of some of his basic emotional problems might precipitate a serious breakdown and it then became imperative not to force this patient to give up drinking before he was psychologically prepared to deal with the tension and anxiety which would then come forth.

REFERENCE

1. FRANCO, S. C.: Problem drinking in industry. Review of a company program. Ind. Med. and Surg. *26:* 5, 221–228, May 1957.

VIII   *Other Industrial Programs for Alcoholism*

THERE ARE several different types of programs in industry for the management of alcoholic employees. One type—a special clinic for alcoholics, separated from the company has been described in detail in the preceding chapter under the heading of the Consolidated Edison-New York University-Bellevue Medical Center Plan.

A second type is represented by the program at Allis-Chalmers Manufacturing Company.[7] For a good many years Allis-Chalmers had recognized that the out-of-control drinker was a problem in the shops and offices. Because of the difficulties that arose from problem drinking, many individuals at the company tried to help these drinkers. Although no oragnized effort was put forth, these volunteers achieved some success. However, as the company increased in size, the problem for management also increased beyond the ability of individuals to cope with it on an unorganized basis. The company, after studying reports on the experiences of other firms and the Yale Clinic, moved ahead to set up a plan of its own. In setting up this plan, help was obtained from a psychologist who did research, arranged tests, drew up forms and procedures, established a reference of material on the subject, a filing system and a general outline for handling the program. It also seemed necessary to have the program in capable hands and controlled by a person thoroughly experienced with the problem of alcoholism and problems of the chronic drinker. A full-time counselor was employed in March of 1949. A former alcoholic himself and formerly executive secretary of Alcoholics Anonymous for Milwaukee county, his advice and ideas were of great value in getting the plan in operation. The plan works in the following way: Shop supervisors make a report to the shop personnel office. The personnel foreman makes arrangements to have the problem drinker referred to the counselor in the personnel service department where the program of treating the illness begins. If the employee requires immediate medical care, the personnel foreman refers him to the company's main hospital and then notifies the counselor. Office supervisors make direct contact with the alcoholic counselor in the personnel service department.

The problem drinker has an opportunity to discuss his problem with the counselor who responds sympathetically and with understanding. Everything that is said is held in the strictest confidence. The counselor also calls at the homes of these employees and talks with their families and friends in an attempt to help the problem drinker. The counselor also is able to obtain hospitalization, clinical diagnosis, psychological tests, and medical examinations when necessary.

Coordinated services are employed in diagnosis and therapeutic techniques. The psychiatrist, physician, psychologist, psychiatric social worker and general counselors all work toward the common goal of understanding and helping the problem drinker. Other company services also are made available to the employee, including legal, housing, medical welfare, veteran counselor, psychological services, mutual aid, credit union, and recreation. In many cases it is necessary to call upon outside agencies, such as hospitals, family, welfare, churches and religious organizations, and Alcoholics Anonymous.

Another type of program is exemplified by the approach of E. I. DuPont De Nemours and Company.[1] They report that since 1943 they have found that the most successful method of handling the alcoholic is with the cooperation and help of Alcoholics Anonymous. Prior to 1943, all kinds of medical programs were tried without any appreciable success. The program in association with Alcoholics Anonymous is rehabilitating 65 per cent of their drinkers. DuPont considers alcoholism as a disease and feels that the rehabilitation of problem drinkers is as much a part of the medical program as any other disease problem. The medical staff includes a member of Alcoholics Anonymous who is not himself a doctor. He has five specific duties. First, he helps in the rehabilitation of any problem drinkers in the Wilmington area. From time to time he is sent to various parts of the country where the DuPont Company has plants, to help in special cases. He helps establish branches of A.A. in locations where the DuPont Company has interests and where no branch exists, and visits various A.A. branches in those parts of the country where the company has plants or units, for the purpose of becoming acquainted with the members of these branches and of acquainting them with the plan procedure in the DuPont Company. He delivers lectures to management, supervisors and workers for the purpose of educating them in the up-to-date and successful methods of treating the alcoholic. By his own efforts and with the help of other employees of the DuPont Company and members of A.A. he tries to discover the problem drinkers as early as possible, especially those we classified as hidden problems.

When it has been determined that an individual is a problem drinker, his immediate supervisor has a talk with him, telling him that he is a medical problem and is being turned over to the medical staff for a period of three months. The employee then reports to the medical staff where considerable time is spent with him, educating him to the fact that he has a disease which is interfering with his business life and his future success, also that his home life is badly disturbed and that the time has come when he must do something about it. He is told that he has three months to prove to the medical staff that he recognizes his own problem, and is anxious to do something about it. He is informed that at the end of three months the medical staff will make recommendations either that he has recognized his problem, is taking it seriously and that in all probability he will be a good employee as far as alcoholism is concerned, or that he does not recognize his problem, shows little or no interest in rehabilitating himself, is not a good risk for the future, and his employment should be terminated.

They instruct the employee that he may pursue any method of cure or relief that he chooses. They do not insist that he join A.A. They do inisist that he be interviewed by a member of A.A. who explains to him how the organization works, what it has done and what it can do for him. They also insist that he attend one A.A. meeting and inform him that from then on it is up to him to choose his method of treatment. He is told he can not have a leave of absence with pay. He can, however, have leave of absence without pay. The above represents their general procedure and has been successful to the extent of 65 per cent, which they regard as 65 per cent better than any other method they have tried.

The approach to the problem drinker by Eastman Kodak Company [3] was to help in the devolment of a community program for education and alcoholism which aimed to make available in industry and in the community all the effective knowledge and techniques which have been developed for the care of the alcoholic. This was a cooperative enterprise involving medicine, psychiatry, social agencies, law enforcement agencies, and Alcoholics Anonymous. In Rochester, since the Committee on Problems of Alcohol of the County Medical Society became active, all the hospitals accept cases of acute alcohol intoxication. There is a clinic for alcoholics established in the Health Bureau under the joint auspices of the Medical Society, the Rochester Committee for Education on Alcoholism, and the Health Bureau. There are over one thousand members of A.A. A special officer in the police department is assigned to work with alcoholics. When a warrant is sworn out for public intoxication, it is served by this man, a member of the local A.A. group. His usual procedure is first to visit the family and discuss the problem, then to visit the employer to find out what kind of worker the problem drinker may be and to enlist his aid; and lastly to call on the man himself; all this before court action is taken. Frequently no court action is necessary, as the understanding way in which this procedure is carried out is an effective introduction to A.A. and rehabilitation.

The Western Electric Company [8] policy regards alcoholism as an illness with service benefits payable when the employee is under proper medical treatment. Medical attention to the acute drinker may vary according to his apparent individual needs. This may include, for the advanced drinker: (1) observation of the employee's state of health—hospitalization may be necessary after a prolonged drinking bout. (2) Alcoholic diagnosis, (3) Counselling, (4) coordination with other company services, (5) referral to one or more outside agencies, (6) follow-up medical and counselling services.

The company's rehabilitation measures are along the following lines:

(1) It is made clear to the employee that it is his own responsibility to achieve complete control of the tendency toward alcoholism, that the company expects he will make favorable progress toward complete rehabilitation and that the company will not tolerate continued interference with job performance.

(2) The employee is urged to avail himself of the recommended agencies, and consideration is given to the possibility of his being helped through his family and church.

(3) Consideration is given to the therapeutic value of transferring the employee to a new job environment during the course of treatment, or of any other desirable adjustment in his work schedule to lessen strain or relieve embarrassment.

(4) Leniency is shown in the event of an occasional relapse, if, during the course of treatment the employee is cooperative, continue to demonstrate a sincere interest in his rehabilitation, and gives evidence of making satisfactory progress.

(5) During the application of rehabilitation measures, disciplinary action is deferred until it is evident that the possibility of obtaining constructive results through the medical department services, which may have included hospitalization, diagnostic procedures, counselling and outside referrals, are remote.

If the employee refuses help or if he fails to show progress after a reasonable period, disciplinary action is then taken.

(1) The company can not retain an habitual non-performer on its rolls, but it may be desirable to temper the process of separation by means of suspensions and leaves of absence in the hope the employee may be shocked into effecting his own rehabilitation before termination of employment becomes necessary.

(2) In deciding upon the particular disciplinary action to be taken, all pertinent factors are taken into consideration; i.e., age, service, kind of job record prior to becoming an alcoholic, remaining potential value to the company, degree of earnestness exhibited in his efforts to assist in his rehabilitation, family conditions, community relationships, etc.

The lack of the right kind of friends and lack of interest in groups, such as lodges, societies and churches is one of the problems of an alcoholic. To help him it is important that he takes an interest in some organization and Alcoholics Anonymous offers this type of group participation. In other cases where there is at least average mental development and good verbal level, referrals are made to Portal House where the employee is counselled under the direction of a psychiatrist and counsellors. (Portal House in Chicago is a community clinic to which industries may refer problem drinkers. A number of industries shared in the creating and supporting this service.) If the family maintains church connections, the pastor can be of help in getting an alcoholic interested in things outside himself, especially in spiritual matters. In other instances, the patient and doctor relationship may appear to be the best form of rehabilitation indicated. Again depending upon the circumstances, there are cases for which state institutions offer the type of treatment necessary to effect rehabilitation.

PROGRAMS IN SMALL COMPANIES

Much can be accomplished by smaller companies in the rehabilitation of alcoholics and the salvaging of valuable personnel despite the lack of a large medical department. The main requirement is that there be at least one person in the company who is keenly interested in the problem. It might be the employer, an employee who is a recovered alcoholic, a part-time physician, or the physician to whom employees are referred for general medical care. Experience has indicated that an ideal arrangement is a twofold approach. It is best for the employer to be the one to kindly but firmly discuss with the employee the difficulties at work created by the drinking. The employee might be given a warning as to loss of job because of his drinking, with the understanding that should drinking that interferes with work recur he will be fired. At the same time, the employee should be offered assistance. This might take the form of referral to a community clinic for alcoholism, a physician who is interested in problems of alcoholism, an employee in the same plant who is a member of Alcoholics Anonymous or directly to Alcoholics Anonymous. On the surface, it may seem unduly harsh to threaten an employee with dismissal. However, in addition to the realities of the difficulties of having an employee who drinks on the job, inefficient work and excessive time loss, realistic pressure by an employer may constitute, for some alcoholics, the only way to convey to the alcoholic the seriousness of his drinking, not only at work but also in terms of his health, family and social life. Although initially one has to expect resentment, a large percentage of alcoholics for whom the job is important will react with gratefulness after abstinence has been achieved. (See CHAPTER V on motivation.) In addition to the benefits likely to accrue to the individual alcoholic from such a program, a consistent adherence to the policy often has a preventative deterrent effect on other potentially alcoholic employees in the same plant.

REFERENCE

1. GEHRMANN, G. H.: The DuPont program for alcoholics. Inventory, *3:* 21–22, 1953.

IX   *Additional Sources of Assistance*

THE YALE PLAN [3]

THE YALE Center of Alcohol Studies has, in the last few years, developed a constructive approach to the problem drinkers in industry. The purposes of the Plan include discovery of the nature, extent and cost of the problem; the development of means to determine what proportion of those affected can be helped; provision of means for such rehabilitation; and the development of increasingly effective methods for discovering cases in earlier stages and at the time of employment. A most important step in realizing these purposes is a program of education to change existing attitudes toward alcoholism and the problem drinker in the environment where he works. When management, supervisors and the workers themselves develop a more sympathetic understanding of the plight of the problem drinker, then the biggest hurdle has been cleared. The problem drinker—the hidden half-man on the production line—will come forward, if he knows that he will receive sympathetic understanding and that his case will be given consideration as a medical disorder.

The Yale Plan is not pointed at drinking itself; individuals naturally resist the attempt to interfere with their personal drinking prerogatives. Paternalism or infringement on the personal rights of the individual under the guise of help will only arouse suspicion and distrust. The treatment of a problem drinker does not involve controversial entanglement in any of the "wet" or "dry" philosophies and arguments, nor is it effective to resort to "preaching," exhortation or the use of scare methods in reaching a satisfactory solution to the individual's problem. The Plan should not become a device for gathering evidence to be used in disciplinary action within an industry. It should be kept on a level above the reach of ridicule of any kind.

For a clearer understanding of problem drinking, it has been suggested that the problem drinker in industry be defined as the employee whose work is materially reduced in efficiency and dependability because of excessive drinking; he is the employee whose drinking excesses are more or less repetitive; he is the employee whose drinking is recognizably affecting his health or personal relations. This is the man who is costing his employer money. This is the man who in many instances can be helped.

The Plan is a flexible program which may be used in whole or in part, depending on the existing policies of the company toward problem drinking, and the size and type of the industry. It is designed to achieve maximum utilization of individual plant facilities. The major steps in the institution of the Yale Plan are as follows:

THE FIRST step in the establishment of the program is to develop understanding of the problem among those in management. They should be acquainted with the nature of alcoholism as a health problem, its extent as it affects industry, and the approved methods of treatment. If the Plan is to succeed, it should have the approval and encouragement of top management. Management should view alcoholism as an illness and a plant health problem.

Material on alcoholism, especially developed for management, is available from the Yale Center of Alcohol Studies. This material should be distributed to those at the highest management level, accompanied by a letter from someone in authority recommending careful reading and consideration.

When sufficient time has passed, it might be advisable to convene a meeting of key personnel openly to consider and discuss the problem.

RESPONSIBILITY FOR the direction of the program, while a matter of company policy, is usually assigned to one of the existing departments of the plant or office. Because problem drinking is primarily a health matter, this responsibility has most frequently been placed with the medical department. In a number of instances, however, where this has not been feasible, responsibility has been given to the personnel or employee relations divisions.

THE NEXT step is to lodge responsibility for carrying out the program. Management may select any person they consider suitably qualified to supervise the operation of a program within their own organization. The individual chosen should have administrative ability and experience in employee counseling, and should be adept at presenting ideas. Above all the program supervisor should look upon the alcoholic as a sick person and should have understanding of his problem. Such a supervisor or other key personnel, once chosen for this responsibility, may attend one of the specialized sessions of the Yale School of Alcohol Studies, where he will gain insight into the problems of alcoholism as they affect the particular industry. A person so chosen and trained should readily handle the details of the program for his company or corporation and supervise its operation under policies determined by the appropriate department.

THE PROGRAM supervisor should set about to mobilize the existing plant facilities that lend themselves readily to furtherance of the program. In a concern of 1500 or more employees, facilities useful for such a program will be available, such as a medical department, a social work staff, an industrial nursing staff, welfare services, a plant counselor, a legal department, a credit union, a recreational supervisor, union representatives, or others. Through the coordination of available plant assets the program may be quickly put into operation without any material addition to the staff.

Where treatment and rehabilitation facilities are lacking within a particular plant, companies may take the opportunity to create such facilities under their own supervision or assume the leadership in establishing them in their communities. It is advisable to evaluate the agencies in the community which are equipped to render services in this field. In the area of diagnosis and treatment, satisfactory working arrangements should be established with physicians, psychiatrists and psychologists specializing in alcoholic cases. Arrangements should be made also with reputable clinics and hospitals that admit alcoholics. Community welfare and social groups should be enlisted. The aid and guidance of the courts and clergy should be sought. Alcoholics Anonymous is a major community asset in the rehabilitation of problem drinkers. As the program advances it may well prove advisable to encourage development of an A.A. group within the plant itself.

As THE program, especially rehabilitation service, is developed, a new conception of the nature and extent of the problem will emerge. At that time the program supervisor can aid in developing a constructive plant policy concerning severance, discipline, retirement, job placement, treatment and rehabilitation.

A MOST important feature of the Plan is counseling and referral. These services should be established for the problem drinker as early as possible. In the early phases of the program the supervisor (with the assistance of the medical and personnel department) will most likely be able to handle this responsibility. As the case load increases—and it will as the program proves its worth—a trained counselor may be required.

The duties of the counselor are threefold, namely, to identify the alcoholic employee who is becoming a problem to himself and to the company; to interpret to him the nature of his problem and the possibility of recovery from the condition; and to refer him to the proper means by which he can be restored to normal working capacity.

If the alcoholic is to be helped he must be viewed realistically. It must be recognized that he can not be expected to correct his condition himself. He needs help. The key to successful counseling is to provide the alcoholic with support and help without necessarily making him aware of his actual dependence, and in a sympathetic, non-critical, non-moralistic manner to aid him in devolping a genuine desire to stop drinking and to bring about a deep conviction that a method is available to him.

Supervisors and administrative personnel have a leading role to play in all phases of this program and will contribute a great deal to the success of the Plan through their improved understanding of the problem of the alcoholic in industry. An education program for these personnel should be established within the plant and should emphasize the vital part each is to play. It is not suggested that the supervisor asume the role of a practiced counselor. Rather, because of his closeness to the employee and his knowledge of his habits and temperament, he should act as liaison between the employee and the responsible division within the plant. Short lectures, motion pictures and selected reading material can be used for this purpose.

Once key personnel have been indoctrinated, personnel can be shown the differences between drinking, drunkenness and alcoholism. Leaflets, pay envelope stuffers, posters, and brief articles in company publications can be used profitably to introduce ideas of prevention of alcohol addiction and to bring about acceptance of treatment by those already suffering from the illness. Such materials have been especially prepared for industry. Already tested for their effectiveness, they can be easily incorporated into a consistent information program for any company or corporation. It should be carefully noted that to be effective such informational programs must be geared to an existing rehabilitation service, must be timed in accordance with a recognized program, and must avoid sensationalism and controversy. As isolated projects such efforts are not usually helpful.

A SURVEY should be made by the program supervisor to ascertain the extent of the problem within the plant. This can be done through techniques developed at the Yale Center which avoid direct questioning or interference with personnel. Initial estimates will probably be on the conservative side since the "hidden man" will not come forward until assured of the Plan's honesty and efficacy. The Allis-Chalmers Company, for example, carried only 70 problem drinkers on its program at first; today it carries some 300. The effectiveness of the program must be continuously investigated if its results are to be ascertained.

THE NATIONAL COUNCIL ON ALCOHOLISM

Located at 2 East 103rd Street, New York 29, New York, The National Council on Alcoholism, a national voluntary agency is a major resource for individuals, groups and organizations seeking information, advice or assistance in dealing with a particular alcoholic patient or the planning of a program for alcoholism. Specific help may be obtained directly or referral will be made to a local committee of this organization. Most of these affiliates of the National Council on Alcoholism maintain Alcoholism Information Centers and some maintain clinics for alcoholics. Local committees are listed under city or county name.

The policy is to further service programs that serve the entire community including business and industry located in a particular area.

The local committee seeks the active participation of representatives of business, industry, and labor in its membership and activities, and in turn expects the organizations they represent to make use of the services and facilities which result from the committee activities. Many companies are currently working with The National Council in this way. To name some of these:

New England Electric
New England Bell Telephone   — Boston Committee on Alcoholism
John Hancock Life Insurance Company

Endicott Johnson I. B. M.	— Broome County (N.Y.) Committee on Alcoholism (Binghamton)
International Harvester Inland Steel Peoples Gas, Light and Coke	— Chicago Committee on Alcoholism
Corning Glass Company Ingersoll-Rand Company	— Corning Area Committee on Alcoholism
Detroit Edison Company	— Detroit Committee on Alcoholism
Prudential Life Western Electric Company	— Essex County (N.J.) Committee on Alcoholism
General Motors (Buick)	— Flint (Mich.) Committee on Alcoholism
Humble Oil Company Hughes Tool Company	— Houston, Texas Committee on Alcoholism
General Electric	— Onandaga Co. Committee on Alcoholism Syracuse, New York
Eastman Kodak Hickey-Freeman Company Bausch Lens Company	— Rochester (N.Y.) Committee on Alcoholism
Youngstown Sheet and Tube Company	— Youngstown (Ohio) Committee on Alcoholism
Morgan Construction Company Norton Company	— Worcester (Mass.) Committee on Alcoholism

ALCOHOLICS ANONYMOUS

This valuable organization has been discussed in CHAPTER V. The address of the nearest A.A. group and literature can be obtained by writing to P. O. Box 459, Grand Central Annex, New York 17, New York. The local group of Alcoholics Anonymous is usually listed in the telephone book.

PORTAL HOUSE

Located at 46 East Superior, Chicago 11, Illinois, Portal House offers to have its staff appear before management officials of a company and explain to them what the alcoholism problem is, what is known about its causes and methods of treatment, what it means to industry, and outline some typical company programs in dealing with this problem. If management is interested in developing a program for their own company, Portal House offers whatever assistance it can in developing the details of the program. They also offer the use of charts and films, as well as a teaching guide on the alcoholism problem and the company program for use by their training department in the education of the foremen and supervisors in the company. When the medical director or other staff members involved in a company have an alcoholic employee whom they deem it advisable to refer, Portal House accepts this employee for diagnosis and subsequent treatment if that is indicated.

REFERENCES

1. HENDERSON, R. M., AND BACON, S. D.: Problem drinking: The Yale plan for business and industry. Quart. J. Stud. on Alcohol. *14:* 247–262, 1953.
2. NORRIS, J. L.: Alcoholism in industry. Quart. J. Stud. on Alcohol. *11:* 562–566, 1950.
3. PFEFFER, A. Z., FELDMAN, D. J., FEIBEL, C., FRANK, J. A., COHEN, M., BERGER, S., FLEETWOOD, M. F., AND GREENBERG, S. S.: A treatment program for the alcoholic in industry. J.A.M.A. *161:* 827–836, June 30, 1956.
4. ——, AND BERGER, S.: Follow-up study of treated alcoholics. Quart. J. Stud. on Alcohol. *18:* 624–658, 1957.
5. Problem drinker in industry, Program of the committee for the study of alcoholism, Milwaukee, Allis-Chalmers Manufacturing Company.
6. SHANNON, F. B.: Absenteeism resulting in loss of production due to problem drinking. Publ. Health News, Trenton, N. J. *34:* 157–159, 1953.

Index